HANDMADE GIFTS *from a* COUNTRY GARDEN

Laura C. Martin

HANDMADE GIFTS from a COUNTRY GARDEN

Principal Photography by
David Schilling

Abbeville Press · Publishers · New York · London · Paris

To my friend and editor, Susan Costello.

Jacket, front, and pages 4–5: Author's garden in spring
Jacket, back: Moss-covered box
Page 1: Violet jelly

Editor: Susan Costello
Designer: Molly Shields
Text Editor: Amy Handy
Production Editor: Abigail Asher
Production Manager: Simone René

ISBN 1-55859-610-0

First edition

Library of Congress Cataloging-in-Publication Data
Martin, Laura C.
     Handmade gifts from a country garden / Laura C. Martin ; principal
photography by David Schilling.
          p.   cm.
     Includes bibliographical references and index.
     ISBN 1-55859-610-0
     1. Nature craft.   2. Herb gardening.   3. Herbs—Utilization.
I. Title.
TT157.M42   1994
745.5—dc20   94-4685
                                                        CIP

All pictures are by Laura C. Martin except the ones listed here, which are by David Schilling: jacket (front and back), 2, 4, 11, 16, 19, 20, 24, 25, 27 (left), 30, 32, 35, 37 (bottom), 39, 42, 44, 46, 50, 52, 54, 55, 56 (bottom), 57 (top), 60, 62, 63, 65 (bottom), 66, 67 (top), 69, 70, 72, 74, 76, 78 (top), 80, 83, 84, 86, 89, 92, 95, 96, 98, 100, 102, 105, 106, 107 (bottom), 108, 110, 112, 113, 115, 117, 118, 120, 121, 127, and 147.

Contents

Gifts for All Seasons

Basic Techniques

Creating a Crafts Garden

Appendixes

Introduction

&

Every time I drive up to my house I look by the front door to see if The Basket is there. The Basket is just an ordinary basket, one I bought at a garage sale years ago. But, of course, it's not the basket itself that brings me tumbling out of the car and bounding up the steps, it's the treasures nestled inside that cause my unbridled enthusiasm.

It became The Basket about ten years ago. My mother was suffering from a bad cold, so I filled my small wicker basket with flowers from my garden and a loaf of homemade bread and took it to her. She was appreciative, and I promptly forgot about the basket until a few weeks later when it reappeared on my doorstep filled with packages of favorite seeds and a new pair of gardening gloves.

Since then The Basket has flown back and forth frequently. Although we sometimes include little baked goods or an occasional piece of chocolate, we most often use it as a vehicle to trade gardening treasures.

During the warm spring months when we are both at a fever pitch of excitement about our gardens, The Basket may change hands several times in one week, depending on supply and request.

Once I put in a few rooted cuttings from my wild clematis vine along with four or five marigold seedlings. Mom returned it to me with several small but healthy tomato plants and—treasure of treasures—a small bag of well-rotted compost.

As the seasons progress, the contents of The Basket change accordingly. Seedlings are replaced by harvest and The Basket gets heavier. During fall, treasures in The Basket change again. A small package of seeds gathered from my meadow accompanies a glorious bouquet of fall-blooming wildflowers.

What we share is more than mere plants and seeds. When I found an exquisite peony blossom in The Basket, I received not only a lovely cut flower but also all the memories that went along with it. It brought to mind images of spring days in my childhood when the peonies were in full bloom and we would cup them in our hands and inhale their sweet perfume. When Mom gets a package of seeds from my meadow, she is receiving not only the seeds but also a tiny dividend for the sacrifices she made when she took care of my children so I could plant a meadow.

To share a garden is to share a lifetime, past, present, and future. Favorite flowers invoke memories of yesterday, give us pleasure today, and give us reason to believe in tomorrow.

Plants that grew and bloomed in my grandma's garden now grow and bloom in my own garden. I hope cuttings from these same plants will take root in the gardens of my children.

If you are blessed with a garden you are also blessed with the opportunity to share it. A giving garden produces a bountiful harvest that can—with a little knowledge and inspiration—be transformed into a multitude of different gifts to be given away. Pleasure in the garden will increase many times over if you share it. Whom you share it with is not as important as the sharing itself. Unless they are given away, garden treasures tend to lose their magic.

The advantages of giving from your garden are many. To give of your garden is to give of yourself—your time, your love, and the sweat of your brow. To give of your garden is to capture the seasons—a clear spring day in a jar of violet jelly, the sweet summer sun in a sachet of dried rose petals, the autumn harvest, or a miniature winter landscape in a glass Christmas ornament.

Gifts from the garden can be as simple as collected seeds of favorite flowers or as complicated and time-consuming as an old-fashioned apple-head doll. These gifts are undeniably unusual and personal. They are, for the most part, inexpensive in terms of money, though not always in terms of time. Many, such as a collection of homemade herbal teas, are quite useful. Others, such as a pot of larkspur, are simply beautiful. Still others, such as a surprise May Day basket found on the doorstep, come so unexpectedly that the recipients may remember them forever.

Handmade Gifts from a Country Garden is a veritable treasure chest of ideas. Each of the sixty gifts is described in detail, and how-to instructions are clear and simple enough to enable even a novice to produce beautiful and exciting gifts. The best kinds of flowers, herbs, and vegetables to grow in your garden for different projects are suggested. There is also information about ways to harvest the produce for the greatest yield from a garden's bounty.

Truth Time, or You, Too, Can Burn Violets

Before I became an author, I always thought that people who wrote books were magicians or wizards, but then I began to wonder. Did their soufflés always turn out perfectly? Didn't they ever have droopy flowers? Didn't they ever hiccup or sneeze? Were these people *real?*

I can't answer for anyone else who writes books, but I can tell you that my experiences in writing this book were very real and that I cried, laughed, stewed, stormed, and, yes, even cursed over many of the crafts in this book.

Take, for example, the day that I gathered up a half-dozen neighborhood kids to pick violets. It really was fun, but it takes a lot of time to pick enough violets to make jelly and a lot of effort to keep six children thinking after a couple of hours that picking violets is still fun. Nevertheless, I came home with enough violet blossoms to make a nice batch of jelly.

I washed the blossoms and immediately put them in a large pan and covered them with water. I wanted them to be as fresh and flavorful as possible. I put the pan on the stove, turned the heat on medium, and ran upstairs to wash up. And then the phone rang. It wasn't until much later that I remembered the violets. They were ruined. All that was left was a black mass in the middle of what was once my favorite pan. I wondered whether I was the only woman in the world who had burned violets that day.

Then there was the time I created a perfect little miniature herb garden. I had it all planted like a tiny English herb garden with pebble walks intersecting four beds planted with mint, thyme, catnip, and oregano. I was pleased and proud as I put it in the den on a table in the front bay window. An hour later I walked back into the den to find pebbles and potting soil and bits of plants strewn all over the floor and my daughter's cat rolling in ecstasy in the catnip. What did I expect? After all, she's a cat.

There was the day that I hosted a fancy spring luncheon and made party favors out of small wicker wheelbarrows planted with real herbs. I carefully watered the herbs to keep them fresh and put them on the table in front of each place setting. They looked great. Twenty minutes later when I filled the water glasses, I found large brown puddles under each herb basket where the water had dripped onto my best linen tablecloth.

Or the day I was getting ready to string vegetables and wanted to dry slivers of corn on the cob before I strung them. It was a sunny day, and I suddenly had the great idea of putting the pieces of corn out in the sun to dry more quickly. I placed them on a tray, found the sunniest spot in the garden, and left them there for several hours. When I returned, the only things remaining were a few kernels and the happy chatter of well-fed squirrels in a nearby tree.

My children, too, had a way of keeping me humble about my crafts. The conversations usually went something like this:

"What's this one supposed to be?"

"Well, it's not really supposed to *be* anything. Just pretty."

"Oh. What happened to it?"

Yes, I photographed only the best of the crafts for this book. I did not photograph the oil that got moldy because I left the herbs in too long, or the rose perfume that smelled like vinegar because I used the wrong fixative, or the peonies that I tried drying in my slightly damp basement.

I am not a magician or a wizard. I am someone, just like you, who loves to work with her hands, loves to create, and loves to give away what I make.

Getting Started

Giving Gifts

&

There is as much of an art to giving gifts as there is to making them. If done correctly, gift giving will be as much fun for the giver as the recipient, and both of you will be pleased, but you can't just give any gift to anybody. Not only should your gifts be beautiful, they should also be appropriate for the recipient.

Although I think my corn-shuck dolls are absolutely darling, it became distressingly clear to me that not everyone wants one on the kitchen windowsill. A friend thought they were "cute" but declined my offer to make one for him. Even holding a golf club? He grinned and suggested that if I wanted to give him a golf club, he'd really prefer a life-size one. However, this same friend is enthusiastically grateful for a jar of fruit jelly or a loaf of herb bread and gives not-so-subtle hints that more would be appreciated.

My mother loves anything made by hand and seems thrilled to receive any kind of craft. She is an outstanding artist herself and understands and appreciates the time and effort that goes into making handcrafted items. Unfortunately, not everyone has an eye trained to value the labor and the tears and toil that sometimes go into making something yourself, so save your treasures for those who do.

You should match up your gifts with your recipients carefully. If your Aunt Julia's house is decorated in a contemporary style with each piece of furniture and fabric conspicuously coordinated, don't give her an apple-head doll dressed in calico and expect her to put it on the mantelpiece. It's just not going to fit.

Be practical about giving your handcrafted items away and try to fit the gift to the person and the situation as best you can. I know few people who would fully appreciate a handmade book of pressed flowers that took ten or twelve hours to make. My sister Linda is one who does, though, so I gave it to her, happily, and in the full knowledge that she will enjoy having it as much as I enjoyed making it for her.

For those people who seem to have everything and need nothing, a handcrafted gift from the garden *may* be the perfect present, particularly at Christmastime. The holidays lend themselves to a more relaxed view of decorating, and people who may not ordinarily get excited about crafts seem to cherish handmade Christmas items. The tiny Victorian tree ornaments made from dried flowers and miniature hats or bits of lace and ribbon are wonderful to give away—they are elegant, inexpensive, and easy to create.

Culinary crafts, also, are always welcomed. I prefer to give away small items, such as little jars of jelly or small loaves of bread or cake. They are just as appreciated as larger items, and by dividing your produce into smaller packages, you'll be able to share it with more people.

Write notes or put labels on your gifts so that the recipient can fully enjoy your present. Bath bags in a basket are wonderful, but, if you mark these according to their intended use (stimulating bath, relaxing bath, bath for aching muscles, and so on), they will be even more useful and appreciated.

Share the symbolism or traditions for some of the gifts you give. I recently went to a friend's housewarming party and took a basket of lily of the valley plants. My friend thanked me and seemed glad to have them, but when she read the note explaining that when a newlywed couple plants lily of the valley in their first garden together it symbolizes renewed love every time it blooms, the small plants took on a whole new meaning for her, and her interest and gratitude increased dramatically.

Make your presentation worthy of the lovely gifts you have crafted. A string of dried flowers laid out in white tissue paper in a long floral box will always look more beautiful than one dumped in the bottom of a paper bag. First impressions are important, and you want the recipients of your gifts to know that you value the gift that you are giving. It takes precious little time and effort and makes a big difference when your gifts are presented beautifully. Attach a label saying what it is and perhaps where you got the ingredients. A jar of jelly, for example, marked "August 1993, Wolf Laurel Pass" is much more intriguing than if it carried a simple tag saying "blackberry jelly." Few people know where Wolf Laurel Pass is, but it doesn't matter. It has the sound of the wilderness and adds a special flavor to the jelly.

Little touches go a long way. Put small pieces of calico on the tops of your jelly jars and tie them with ribbon, find an inexpensive basket to put jars of pepper oil in, and save tiny, interesting jars to fill with bath oils.

Above all, don't deprecate or make excuses for your gifts, even to yourself. Anyone who puts time and effort into making something by hand is an artist, no matter what the finished product looks like. If a particular craft doesn't exactly turn out the way you thought it might, keep it yourself, because you will appreciate what went into it perhaps better than anyone else. I have several lopsided dolls and lumpy wreaths; these are my foster children that I love and cherish and would not give away for anything.

You don't have to be trained or be particularly talented or creative to be an artist. All you have to do is love what you're doing. The more you do, the better you'll get at it. You can certainly do each of these crafts by yourself. None *require* the presence of two people, but half the fun of doing crafts and projects is in sharing them. Crafting with friends is fun—it keeps everything in perspective, both your triumphs and your disasters. There are many ways to share crafts. You can take a class, join a workshop, teach someone else, or simply invite over a group of friends and spend the afternoon making things. Ideas will multiply and creativity will feed on itself with many minds working together.

Each of us has gifts within ourselves that we are longing to share. I hope that *Handmade Gifts from a Country Garden* helps you to discover those treasures.

How to Use This Book
&

Making gifts from the bounty of your garden can be fulfilling, but it can also be challenging if you don't have the proper tools and equipment. For the most part, the techniques and skills needed for most of these crafts can be learned easily. Although some of the projects are a bit time-consuming and others take a fair amount of dexterity, there are many crafts that are basically just good ideas that take little time, money, or skill, and a minimum of equipment.

Time

The time involved in each project is listed. The times given do not include gathering plant material. Times will vary considerably from one person to another, depending on skill and interest level. A time-consuming project is not necessarily a difficult one. For example, it is easy to push boxwood into a Styrofoam ball, but it takes a few hours to cover the ball completely.

Cost

The cost for each project is based on homegrown plant material and does not include the cost of purchasing tools. If you have to purchase flowers or herbs, it may greatly alter the cost. For example, two dozen roses dried from your garden cost you nothing, but two dozen roses dried and purchased from a craft store may cost more than fifty dollars. The cost for each project is given in symbols: Projects costing less than $5.00 to make are indicated by one star (☆); ☆☆ indicates a cost of about $6.00 to $10.00; ☆☆☆ means $11.00 to $20.00; ☆☆☆☆ means materials may cost over $20.00.

From time to time, most of us will probably have to supplement what we can grow with what we can buy. I can't grow roses very well in my own garden, because I don't get enough sun. Rather than buy full-grown and very expensive dried roses, I purchase dried sweetheart roses, which are less expensive and are almost as beautiful and certainly as charming. Occasionally, the time involved in using homegrown plant products may simply not be worth it. I know that I can make essential oils and floral water, but it is a long, involved process, and I choose to buy these readymade instead.

You can do every craft in this book without setting foot in a garden. Plants and flowers, fresh and dried, are readily available in nearly every part of the country. If it is using the products of the garden rather than gardening itself that interests you, then by all means do what you enjoy most.

Difficulty

The difficulty rating for each craft discussed is indicated with symbols ranging from ✂, meaning a seven-year-old child could do it, up to ✂✂✂✂, indicating that it takes good hand-eye coordination, some fine motor skills, and usually a lot of patience. As you do these crafts, the difficulty level, as well as the time required, will lessen. Just be patient and persistent until you are pleased with the results.

Shelf Life

The shelf life listed for each project indicates an approximate life span for that particular craft. Some of these gifts, such as the corn-shuck angels, will last forever. Others, such as the whole wheat basil bread, will last only a few days.

Notes

Often, as part of the introduction to a project, I point out mistakes and problems that I experienced while doing that craft. I'm sure that you will encounter your own set of problems—it comes with doing crafts—but I hope these notes will help you avoid some trouble spots.

Variations

The variations given at the end of some projects are merely suggestions for other ways that you can use or do these projects. I've listed just a few; the variations and possibilities are limited only by your own imagination and resources.

Basic Techniques

Many of the craft projects require a few easily learned techniques. Mastery of these basic skills will enhance your crafts and make working with them even more enjoyable.

Gardening

Notes on specific plants and their growing requirements will help you create a garden of flowers, herbs, vegetables, and shrubs that will be useful for many of these crafts.

Appendixes

The appendixes are included to make it easier to create and use these gifts. Here you will find the projects grouped by occasion (bridal showers, Mother's Day gifts, housewarming presents, and so on), by type (food items or Victoriana, for example), and suggestions for cost- and time-effective projects that are ideal for selling at bazaars and fund raisers. Sources for materials and plants are listed as well.

Essential Equipment

The right tools and equipment will make the creation of your projects go smoothly. Knowing what you need before you get started will lessen wasted time and help you avoid frustration.

None of the crafts listed require sophisticated tools or machinery. These are gifts that are easy to make with a minimum amount of trouble. Most of the supplies and materials are readily available in garden centers or in craft or fabric stores. A good hardware store can supply you with the basic tools you need.

If you don't have one already, find a box to hold your tools. Depending on your needs, this can range from a cardboard box to a lockable metal tool cabinet. If you keep all your tools in one place it will save time and frustration in the long run.

FLOWER PRESS: Presses come in a variety of types and sizes. The easiest to use open like a book with screws on one side and some sort of clasp on the other side so that the press can be tightened down firmly. Flower presses can be made easily or can be purchased from a nature or craft store.

Some of the most widely used presses are made of two pieces of wood on either side of a stack of blotting paper. Screws are found at each corner. The disadvantage of using this type is that each corner must be unscrewed completely and the entire press disassembled every time plants are either put in or taken out.

Books make an easy, quick press. They are (one hopes) in every home, and can hold small to medium-size plants. If you press plant materials in a book, place them between pieces of blotting paper and then slip this between the pages of the book. To hasten the drying process, place other books on top of the one used as a press.

GLUE GUNS: Purists rarely use a glue gun, saying that the glue dries too quickly and interferes with the artistic process, but for quick fixes and for hard-to-hold materials, a glue gun is a wonderful tool.

Glue guns use a small stick of waxlike glue that is heated up then released by pulling a small trigger. The glue comes in various sizes and colors. Less-expensive guns without the trigger mechanism, which work by pushing the glue stick through the gun, can also be bought. They are not as useful, however, because it is difficult to stop and start the flow of glue quickly.

HAMMERS: A curved-claw hammer is the most useful kind of hammer. The claw serves to remove nails. To drive them home, grasp the hammer at the end of the handle. Hold the nail between your thumb and forefinger and tap lightly a few times until the nail is embedded in the wood enough to stand up by itself. Then remove your fingers and drive the nail.

Tack hammers are small, lightweight hammers used for driving in tacks or small nails.

KNIVES: A basic pocketknife is easier (and safer) to carry in the garden than scissors and is often a more efficient cutting tool. An old butter knife is useful for spreading glue. A sharp, long-bladed knife can be used to cut floral foam.

PRUNING SHEARS: These come in a wide variety of styles and prices. Choose the best you can afford and keep them sharp. Dull shears sometimes cause damage to stems and branches, which may lead to disease later on.

SCISSORS: Keep at least two pairs of scissors, one for cutting fabric and one for cutting everything else. If you use fabric scissors for cutting paper, they will soon be so dull they won't even cut fabric. A sturdy pair of kitchen scissors will cut a variety of things including paper, plant stems, corn shucks, and light wire.

WIRE CUTTERS: Wire cutters are necessary for all but the thinnest strands of wire.

Helpful Materials

&

STUFFING: Batting or stuffing, made from cotton or synthetics, can be found in any craft or quilting shop. Batting usually comes in rolls, while stuffing is a mass of materials, easily pulled apart.

CONTAINERS: Baskets can be made of a tremendous variety of materials and can range in price from a few pennies to quite expensive. Although fine baskets make elegant gifts,

inexpensive baskets found at the supermarket or discount store can often be dressed up and make good containers for your gifts from the garden. These baskets can also be lined with a waterproof material (even a plastic trash bag can be cut to fit the bottom of a basket) so that they can be planted with live plants.

Glass jars and bottles are used to hold pretty herb vinegars and oils, bath oils, jelly, and jam.

Pottery or crockery is useful for holding large bouquets of flowers or dried plant material.

FABRICS: Cheesecloth, a loosely woven cotton fabric, is used for many herb crafts including tea bags, bath bags, and *bouquet garni*. The loose weave makes it good for crafts where materials need to be held together but where the flavor or fragrance should be easily released.

Muslin is a good, basic fabric useful for dyeing projects, as the base for a pillow, or as a substitute for cheesecloth.

Since muslin is usually sprayed with a fabric treatment, it should be washed before use.

Lace and brocade are fabrics used for Victorian crafts such as sachets. These can be as elegant and expensive as desired. Calico or gingham can be filled with herbs or potpourri to create a country look.

GLUE AND ADHESIVES: White household glue has multiple uses and will be good to have on hand. Be sure to choose a variety that dries clear. Spray adhesives are also available and are good for covering delicate or hard to reach areas.

MOSS: Sphagnum moss is made of dense plant fibers that smell like the bog from which they come. This is a wonderful material for filling wreath or topiary forms. It will absorb its weight in water many times over and retains moisture for a long time.

Sheet moss is a thin layer of moss used to cover topiary or Styrofoam forms for various crafts.

Spanish moss is gray-green and curly and is often used at the base of an arrangement or in a wreath to cover up the mechanics.

PEBBLES AND GRAVEL: Available from garden-supply stores, these are used in the bottom of containers to help the soil drain better. Clean stream pebbles are also used decoratively at the tops of pots or as paths in miniature potted gardens.

PLANTING MATERIALS: Commercial potting soil should be used for most crafts that require planting. Although you can go out and dig up part of your garden to get soil, it is not always very fertile or clean and sometimes causes more problems than it is worth.

RIBBON: Ribbon will add grace and beauty to many crafts. Luckily, many kinds of ribbons are available to the crafty gardener—everything from very inexpensive paper ribbon to fine silk ribbon that sells for ten dollars (£7) a yard (m) or more.

One of the most effective and easiest to use is ribbon that is wired along both edges. The thin wire, hidden by the ribbon, makes it easy to form many shapes. Bows will stay exactly where you place them. In addition, you can make the ribbon tails wave or flow as necessary.

Inexpensive paper ribbon often comes in colorful patterns and is useful in such crafts as the pressed-flower picture. Pastel satin ribbons can be used to decorate May baskets, the pressed-flower book, and tiny Easter baskets that go on the Easter brunch buffet table.

Note that ribbon widths as given in the lists of materials may be approximate. Very slight variations in width will not affect the overall appearance of the finished project.

WIRE: This comes in many different gauges and lengths. It can be bought on spools or reels, and in the United States in cut lengths (usually 12 or 18 inches). The gauge—light, medium, or heavy—refers to how stiff and thick the wire is. An 8 gauge can be bent easily and is thin enough to cut with scissors. A 16 gauge is quite stiff and needs to be bent with a pair of pliers.

FOR FLOWER ARRANGING

CHICKEN WIRE: This is useful in topiary as well as in arranging flowers. A ball of chicken wire pushed down into a container will hold the stems of flowers upright.

FLORAL PICKS: These are small wooden sticks, a little larger than a toothpick, usually painted green. Attached to the sticks are thin pieces of wire. Floral picks are used to wire weak or fragile stems of fresh or dried flowers to something a bit more stable for inserting into various materials.

FLORAL TAPE: A slightly stretchy brown, green, or white tape, this is used in floral arrangements. It has a variety of purposes but is most often used to wrap a stem that has been wired to a floral pick.

OASIS: This is a lightweight, dense foam, different from Styrofoam. It will quickly absorb its weight in water many times over. The foam should be cut to fit snugly in a container. If the fit is not tight enough, the top may become heavier than the bottom and could tip the arrangement over.

WATER VIALS: These small, narrow tubes with perforated lids are used as portable vases and are wonderful for keeping plant material fresh-looking for a long time. They can be used in miniature gardens or in baskets.

FOR DRYING FLOWERS

Many materials readily absorb moisture, making them useful for drying various plant material. Sand has been used for this purpose for centuries. One part sand to two parts borax is still used today, though this mixture will sometimes stick together, becoming heavy and damaging delicate blossoms.

The best desiccant to use is silica gel, a commercially available drying agent that can absorb forty times its weight in water. It will dry plant material in just a few days, helps retain the original color, is lightweight, and will not damage the flowers.

FOR MAKING JELLY

- Large, flat-bottomed kettle
- Large tongs for removing jars from water bath
- Large, tall pan, or pot, for processing jars

FOR DYEING FABRICS, WOOL, AND YARN

- Large kettle of stainless or enameled steel
- Wooden spoons for stirring the dye bath and handling the fibers
- Mesh strainer for separating the plant material from the dye bath
- Thermometer for measuring the temperature of the bath

FOR TOPIARY

Wire frames are the basis for indoor mock topiary. These can be bought at a garden-supply or crafts store and come in many different shapes and sizes. Popular animal shapes include bears and turtles. Geometric shapes include cones, Christmas trees, balls, and wreaths. You can also make your own shapes by bending chicken wire into the desired design.

Monofilament fishing line is useful in securing sheet moss to the topiary frame. Do not use blue line, which will detract from the natural look of your topiary. Clear line is used most often, but dark green line is also used successfully.

FOR MAKING PAPER

- Blender for making pulp out of waste paper and plant fibers
- Mould and deckle for gathering the pulp and separating it from the liquid
- Iron to give the paper a smooth finish

Gifts for All
Seasons

Primrose

The name primrose is
thought to mean
"most excellent."

Fairies are said to take
shelter under primrose
leaves during a
rainstorm.

The German word for
this is " little keys
to heaven."

Spring in southern regions is unlike spring anywhere else in the world. It may be a carpet of violets, a canopy of dogwoods, a promise come true as the earth bursts forth into an abundance of beauty. Unlike our northern neighbors, we have not been snowbound for months, so spring is not so much a release from dreary cold weather as it is a time to stand and wonder at the glory of nature. ❧ Spring is a time for discovering. It is a time for playing a gentle game of hide and seek, lifting a winter blanket of mulch to see what is awake and ready to begin the cycle of growth in the garden once again. ❧ There is

Spring Surprises

probably nothing quite like finding the first flower of spring. Perhaps it is a small crocus peeking up through the cold February ground, or it might be bloodroot or hepatica bravely blooming in the middle of a chilly, quiet forest. Whatever the size, shape, or color of this flower, it warms the heart and cheers the soul. ❧ For the gardener with an abundance of flowers, or for anyone with an abundance of happy spirits, spring is a time of sharing. From the surprise and delight of an unexpected May Day basket to the pride and pleasure of a special book of pressed flowers, spring gifts bring joy and are lovely mementos of this season of new beginnings.

Potpourri

For months I save bits and pieces of petals and leaves for my potpourri. Potpourri is the crazy quilt of the crafty gardener. Just as an old-fashioned quilt will be made of scraps of clothing from every member of the family, a good mixture of this sensuous, richly scented mixture should tell a little something about you and those close to you.

Potpourri has become somewhat of a tradition among my friends and family. They know that I have an insatiable desire for additions to my potpourri bag, but they have learned through the years that these additions have to be meaningful. Even if a flower dries well and holds its scent, it may not be added to my potpourri. I collect bits and pieces of memories, not just a mass of dried plant material.

Running my hands through the petals I've been saving for the past half year, I am momentarily lost in recollection. Pieces of gold and yellow pansies bring vivid memories of my annual May Day party and the baskets we decorated. White rose petals are from my sister's wedding, the pink ones from my daughter's thirteenth birthday, red ones from a friend at Christmas. Small bits of red cockscomb came from my mother's garden, and tiny heads of globe amaranth were gathered at a friend's home in the mountains.

Into this bag of memories go petals from my nephew's christening and my parents' anniversary party. Flowers seem to be an integral part of every major celebration and potpourri offers a beautiful way to keep memories of these happy times. It is family history in a bag, friendship in a pouch.

For centuries we have captured the scents of herbs and flowers and brought them indoors to enjoy. Whether we simply pick a jar full of roses for the kitchen table or carefully dry individual stalks of lavender for the bath, we take great pleasure in fragrance from the garden.

During medieval times these scents were even more important than they are today. Sanitary practices were not always part of everyday life, and streets—sometimes even homes—were filled with unpleasant odors. Women often carried small bags of scented herbs to hold to their noses as they walked the street, hence the term *nosegay*.

Potpourri is a mixture of dried petals and herbs combined for their fragrance and color. There are two main kinds of potpourri, moist and dry. While moist mixtures retain their fragrance for much longer periods of time, dry potpourri are much easier and quicker to make and, being more attractive, are often displayed in glass jars or open bowls or containers.

A fixative, usually orris root, is added to the petals and plant parts to help the scent last longer. Without this fixative, the fragrance of the potpourri would fade quickly. Essential oil made from various flowers and herbs is also added to the mixture. This enhances and amplifies the scent.

Although many complicated recipes exist for making beautiful potpourri, the basic process is relatively easy and need not be confusing or time-consuming. The mixtures can be dry or moist and can be made to feature any number of dominant scents, such as sweet, spicy, woodsy, or citrusy.

The following flowers and herbs are useful in creating a mixture. Carefully blend scents that are pleasing to you and that seem to be in the same general fragrance family.

SWEET: Chamomile · Daffodil (small) · Gardenia · Lavender · Lilac · Lily of the valley · Marigold · Rose · Sweet pea · Violet

SPICY: Allspice · Carnation · Cinnamon · Ginger · Mint · Vanilla beans

WOODSY: Hemlock · Pine · Rosemary · Spruce · Sweet woodruff · Thyme

CITRUSY: Bee balm · Florida azalea · Lemon balm · Lemongrass · Lemon peel · Lemon verbena · Orange peel · Scented geraniums (lemon, orange, pineapple)

TIME: 1 hour (after plant material has been dried)

LEAD TIME: 8 weeks from fresh flowers to ripe potpourri

COST: ☆ (for orris root and essential oils)

MATERIALS:

4–6 cups (1–1.5 liters) dried scented flower petals and herbs (at least half should be rose petals)

1 cup (250 ml) small flower heads or blossoms for color and texture

2 tablespoons powdered orris root

4–5 drops essential oil (a small bottle of essential oil will make gallons of potpourri)

DIFFICULTY: ✂ ✂

SHELF LIFE: Scent should last 2–3 years.

See Basic Techniques (page 124) for guidelines on drying flowers and herbs.

1. Combine ingredients in a very large bowl.
2. Mix with your hands, turning the materials over and over until well blended.
3. Place in an airtight container in a dark, cool place and allow to mellow for 6 weeks. To make sure the scents blend well, shake or mix every few days.
4. After 6 weeks the potpourri is ready to use and can be put

into sachet bags, left in an open dish, or placed in a specially designed potpourri container. Potpourri will lose its scent more quickly if left in an open dish.

Variations: Many different kinds of potpourri can be created based on similar scents or colors. Try the following combinations.

Rosy Red Potpourri

3 cups (750 ml) red rose petals and buds

1 cup (250 ml) pink rose petals

¼ cup (60 ml) red cockscomb

¼ cup (60 ml) red globe amaranth blossoms

2 tablespoons powdered orris root

4 drops rose essential oil

Note: To turn this into a Christmas potpourri, add sprigs of dried rosemary and pine needles.

Lavender Blue Potpourri

2 cups (500 ml) dried lavender flowers

1 cup (250 ml) white rose petals

½ cup (125 ml) bachelor's button flower heads

½ cup (125 ml) blue pansies

2 tablespoons powdered orris root

4–5 drops lavender essential oil

Sachets

Sachets are small bags filled with crumbled potpourri. These bags can be made from any fabric that has a loose enough weave to allow the scent to escape. It can be as simple as

Moss-Covered Box

☙

During the afternoon in the early-spring woods pale sunshine flits between the trees, then, quickly tiring, slips back into the shadows to sleep again. The woods are clean and barren, with few plants braving the March cold. Because there is no competition for attention, moss on the forest floor takes on a new beauty.

Sheet moss holds a hundred uses for the crafty gardener. It is an all-purpose covering for many different kinds of gifts and crafts. One of the easiest is simply to cover a cardboard or plywood container with the moss to create a lovely woodsy box.

TIME: 30 minutes

COST: ☆ (for box)

MATERIALS:

    Cardboard or plywood box, with lid

    Thin sheet moss

    Craft glue

    Dried rosebud and baby's breath

DIFFICULTY: ✄ ✄

SHELF LIFE: Indefinite

gingham or muslin, or as elegant as brocade or silk. The bags can be any size, but small ones have a certain charm and are useful for slipping into a chest of drawers.

Sachets make terrific little presents that can be given anytime during the year. Keep a supply of small bags on hand, fill them with potpourri, tie with a ribbon, and voilà—instant gift.

1. Cut 2 pieces of fabric 7 inches (18 cm) long and 5 inches (13 cm) wide. Put the pieces right sides together, and stitch across the bottom and up two sides. Finish the top edge by cutting with pinking shears, hemming, or doing a zigzag stitch on the sewing machine.
2. Turn right side out, fill with crumbled potpourri, and tie at the top with ribbon.

1. Measure the height and the width or circumference of your box (photo A, page 26).
2. Cut a piece of very thin sheet moss (photo B, page 26) as long as the width or circumference, and as wide as the height of the box, *minus 1 inch (3 cm) off the height* (this allows the top to close snugly).
3. Apply a line of glue along the sides of the box, close to the bottom. Apply another line of glue 2 inches (5 cm) from the top of the box, making sure to leave plenty of room for the top to fit easily.
4. Carefully place the moss over the glue on the box.

A

B

C

9. Fill the box with potpourri, or leave it empty to be filled with other treasures. A heart-shaped box filled with sweet-smelling potpourri makes a wonderful Valentine's box for just about anyone.

Topiary Bear

High up by the window in the pink and green bathroom of my friend Sally's beautiful Victorian house sits a little empty shelf. It just seems to be waiting for a small topiary bear. Even in an urban office a topiary bear, nestled among computers, is a pleasing reminder of the countryside.

Stuffed and planted topiaries are popular in garden stores and come in many different animal shapes, from turtles to ducks to bears. Unfortunately, they are usually expensive—even small ones can cost thirty dollars (£20). But the forms are easy to plant and, if planted with something as forgiving as fig vine, are easy to grow and maintain to add a bit of whimsy to the indoor garden. Fig vine is a wonderful choice because it withstands neglect and poor light conditions cheerfully.

An alternative to the vine-covered topiary is one covered with daisies, which is especially nice for baby showers instead of a traditional flower arrangement.

Topiary frames for home use come in a variety of shapes, or you can create your own out of chicken wire. The challenge in making a small stuffed topiary is in keeping the shape tight enough to be recognizable; this is easier if you use small flowers.

TIME: 45 minutes to 1 hour
LEAD TIME: 6 weeks
COST: ☆☆ to ☆☆☆
MATERIALS:
   Topiary frame
   Sphagnum moss

5. Tie with a string or ribbon (temporarily) to keep the moss firmly attached to the box until the glue dries (photo C).
6. Repeat for the top, cutting a piece of moss slightly larger than the top of the box and pulling the sides down to cover the edges of the top. If the top has deep sides, it may be necessary to cover these with a separate piece.
7. When the top has dried, decorate it by gluing on a small dried red rosebud and a tiny sprig of baby's breath.
8. To make it easier to open the box, glue a small loop of ribbon to the inside of the box, extending it so that it can be easily grasped from the outside when the box is closed.

Fishing line

Fig vine or other small-leaved vine that requires very
    little light

DIFFICULTY: ✄ ✄ ✄

SHELF LIFE: Several years, if cared for properly

1. Soak a 10-ounce (280 g) bag of sphagnum moss in a sink or large bowl until saturated.
2. Drain excess water from the moss, then carefully stuff the moss into the frame (photo A). The wet moss will stick together, but tying thin wire or clear filament (fishing line) around the frame helps keep the moss in place.
3. Remove fig vine from container and carefully separate it into many small bundles, making sure to have plenty of roots with each bundle of leaves.
4. Using your finger, a stick, or a pencil, create small cavities in the moss and insert the roots of the vine. Repeat until the

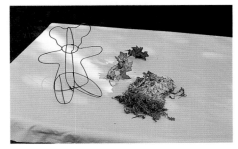

A

B

vine is planted evenly throughout the frame (photo B). Don't expect the vine to cover the frame at this point; you'll be able to see a lot of the moss.

5. Take very thin wire and cut many 2-inch (5 cm) pieces. Bend these in half (they will look like miniature hairpins) and stick them into the moss, effectively securing the vine to the moss and frame.
6. The trick is to keep the vine growing all over the frame. For the bear, the difficult parts are the extremities—the nose, ears, and front paws. The topiary can generally sit in a tray of water. To get moisture to the outer areas, treat it to a bath in the sink or a tub of water once a week.

Variation: For the daisy-covered bear (see page 159) you'll need 30–50 flowers (florist's daisies or chrysanthemums come about 6–8 flowers per stalk). Follow steps 1 and 2 above. Cut the flower stems so that the flowers will be flush with the frame when the stems are 2–3 inches (5–8 cm) into the moss. Cover the frame with flowers, using contrasting flowers to make the facial features.

Violet Jelly

&

I gathered up the neighborhood children for our annual violet-picking party. This is a wonderful activity to do with kids. As my little friend Kate put it, "It's better than picking blueberries 'cause when you drop them, they don't roll."

Hand out small lunch bags to as many children as you're willing to take on and find a violet-filled spot that you are *certain* has not been sprayed with any kind of chemical. You only need the tops of the violets to make jelly, so tell the children to pluck off just the blossoms.

It takes a lot of violets to make jelly, but you'll be surprised how quickly you can gather enough with an enthusiastic band of violet-pickers. In case you don't have children available and you get bone-weary of picking tiny violets all by yourself, you can always "fill in" with blue or purple pansies.

The jelly itself is a color impossible to duplicate, either naturally or synthetically. Violets make a clear, reddish-purple jelly, a color as difficult to describe as it is to imitate.

TIME: 1 hour
COST: ☆
MATERIALS:
    Approximately 5 cups (1.25 liter) of violet petals
    Sugar
    1¾ oz. (49 g) powdered fruit pectin (1 package)
    Small jelly jars
DIFFICULTY: ✂ ✂
SHELF LIFE: Indefinite

1. Gather violet petals and place in a large, flat saucepan and cover with water. Simmer for 20 minutes, or until color is gone from petals.
2. Drain off the plant material, saving the juice.
3. Measure the juice. For every 2 cups (500 ml) of juice add 2 cups (500 ml) of sugar and a package of powdered fruit pectin. Pour into hot, sterilized jars and process for 10 minutes. (See Basic Techniques [pages 125–26] for general instructions on making jelly.)
4. Remove from processor and let cool.
5. Test to make sure the tops have sealed (see page 126).

Violet-Jelly Shortbread

&

Although violet jelly is wonderful simply spread on toast or English muffins, it also makes an interesting and unusual cookie in the form of Violet-Jelly Shortbread, a perfect gift for someone who has everything.

TIME: 30 minutes
COST: ☆
MATERIALS:
    ½ cup (125 ml) butter
    ½ cup (125 ml) sugar

1¼ cups (315 ml) all-purpose flour

⅓ cup (80 ml) violet jelly

2 large eggs

½ cup (125 ml) brown sugar

1 teaspoon vanilla

2 tablespoons flour

pinch salt

⅛ teaspoon baking soda

1 cup (250 ml) pecans, chopped

DIFFICULTY: ✄

SHELF LIFE: Up to 6 months in the freezer

1. Mix butter, sugar, and flour until it is the consistency of fine meal. Press into the bottom of greased 9-inch (22.5 cm) square pan. Bake at 350° F (177° C) for 20 minutes, or until edges are lightly browned.
2. Remove from oven and spread violet jelly generously over the shortbread.
3. Beat together eggs, brown sugar, vanilla, 2 tablespoons flour, salt, baking soda, and pecans. Spread evenly over the jelly and shortbread.
4. Return to oven and bake 20 minutes longer, or until top mixture is set.
5. Cool in pan and cut into bars.

Pressed-Flower Picture

⚘

Marveling at the perfection of a tiny Johnny-jump-up, I had an urge to *do* something with it. Too small to make much of an arrangement, it was added to my book of pressed flowers.

Pressing flowers is the perfect answer to this urge to *do*. Spring flowers seem to lend themselves well to the art of pressing. They are generally smaller than summer or autumn blooms and have thin petals and center parts, all of which make them excellent subjects for pressing.

One of my favorite handmade crafts is a quilt I made fifteen years ago. It is composed of twenty white squares with a wildflower embroidered or appliquéd on each one. I wanted a similar look, without spending months and years doing it, so I created a miniature "quilt" picture using pressed flowers and strips of floral ribbon. I sent this to a favorite friend in New York, who has it hanging in her office. It lends a touch of elegant country to her sophisticated city office.

TIME: 3 hours

LEAD TIME: A few days to 2 weeks

COST: ☆☆ to ☆☆☆

MATERIALS:

　Ruler

　9 × 12-inch (22.5 × 30-cm) piece of heavy white water-color paper

2½ yards (2.3 m) ⅝-inch (1.3-cm) wide floral ribbon

Craft glue

12 pressed flowers

12 × 14-inch (30 × 35-cm) piece of blue poster board

12 × 14-inch (30 × 35-cm) frame

DIFFICULTY: ✂ ✂

SHELF LIFE: Years, although some flowers may begin to
fade after about 6 months

1. Using a ruler, divide the white watercolor paper into 12
   equal squares in 4 rows of 3: mark across the top of
   the page at 3 inches (7.5 cm) and at 6 inches (15 cm),
   and mark at 3, 6, and 9 inches (7.5, 15, and 22.5 cm) along
   the edge.
2. Cut 4 pieces of ribbon 12 inches (30 cm) long and 5 strips
   9 inches (22.5 cm) long. Glue one long piece down at the
   3-inch (7.5 cm) and one at the 6-inch (15 cm) mark, and
   glue one piece at each of the 3-, 6-, and 9-inch (7.5-, 15-, and
   22.5-cm) marks. Reserve the remaining pieces for step 6.
3. Choose 12 pressed flowers and leaves (photo A) and put
   one in each square you created. Move them around until
   you are pleased with the balance and symmetry of the piece
   (photo B).
4. When you are satisfied with the placement, put a tiny spot
   of glue under each flower or leaf to secure it to the paper.
5. Center the white watercolor paper on the larger piece of
   blue poster board, measuring to get even margins (photo C).
   Secure with spots of glue at each corner.
6. Glue the remaining pieces of ribbon to cover the outer edges
   of the white paper. Write the name of each flower in a corner of each square.
7. After the piece has dried for 30 minutes or more, place in
   the frame.

*Variation: Use different-colored backgrounds and other flowers to cre-
ate a different look. Rose-colored flowers intersected with thin black
ribbon on a black border will create a stained-glass effect, which will
be further enhanced if you curve the top edges into an arch.*

A

B

C

Floral Hat

❧

My favorite party of the year is my annual spring garden party.
Sisters, mother, friends, and I dress in our own private version
of the English "frock," but the dresses cannot compare to the
beauty of the hats that each of us decorates to wear that day.
The creations range from pillbox to sombrero, but whatever

the size, each is beautiful in its own right, dripping with flowers and ribbons.

To make a lasting gift of a floral hat you will have to use dried instead of fresh flowers, but the basic technique is the same. Use lots of ribbons and an abundance of flowers and your head will never look prettier. If you use fresh flowers, though, watch out for the bees, for you'll be irresistible.

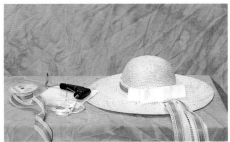

A

B

TIME: 1 hour

LEAD TIME: overnight, to condition some of the flowers

COST: ☆☆ to ☆☆☆

MATERIALS:

Fresh flowers

Hat (straw sun hats are the easiest to work with and are readily available at Eastertime in discount and craft-supply stores)

Ribbon:

2½ yards (2.25 m) 2-inch (5-cm) wide white picot-edged ribbon (enough to go around the brim of the hat, make a bow, and hang down the back)

2½ yards (2.25 m) 2-inch (5-cm) wide pink ribbon with white edge

2 yards (1.8 m) ⅜-inch (.7-cm) wide white ribbon (enough to tie 6 or 7 small bundles of flowers)

Glue gun and glue stick (all-purpose household glue can be used instead but is more difficult to work with because it takes so long to dry)

DIFFICULTY: ✄ ✄ ✄

SHELF LIFE: Hats decorated with dried flowers should last indefinitely. Fresh-flower hats will last only a few hours. To extend the life of a fresh-flower hat, mist with an atomizer, cover loosely with a large plastic bag, and store in the refrigerator.

1. Cut a length of 2-inch (5-cm) wide white ribbon long enough to go around the base of the hat; glue it down flat against the hat, with the two ends meeting in the back.

C

2. Cut a piece of contrasting ribbon the same length and glue over white ribbon.

3. From the white ribbon, make a flat bow with long tails (see Basic Techniques, page 125) and glue to the back of the hat (photo A).

4. Select small bunches of flowers and tie together with strips of ⅜-inch (.7-cm) wide ribbon (photo B).

5. When you have 6 or 7 small flower bundles tied, begin placing them around the base of the hat as if you are creating a wreath around the base (photo C). Be sure that all the flowers point in the same direction and that the stems of one

bunch are effectively hidden by the flowers of the next. Keep arranging and rearranging until you are pleased with the composition.

6. Using a glue gun, attach the small bunches of flowers. Glue the small ribbon ties to the ribbon on the hat, rather than gluing the actual flower stems, which will wilt from the heat of the glue gun.

Variation: The same procedure can be used with small bunches of dried flowers. A hat decorated with ribbons and dried flowers can be hung on a bedroom wall, in the powder room, or over the mantel to bring a touch of Victorian beauty to any home.

Bride's Book of Flowers

When my sister was married last fall, I wanted to give her a keepsake present, something that would remind her of her wedding, truly a happy celebration. I decided to make her a Bride's Book of Flowers. This includes small pressed flowers from her bridal bouquet, and choice blossoms from arrangements and decorations from parties given for her, as well as a few flowers of particular symbolism, such as crocus, which is said to inspire romance between lovers.

I began collecting small flowers from each party, carefully taking a few blossoms at the end of the occasion. Although color and form were important, equally significant were the symbolism and meaning of the different flowers. Luckily, small flowers are best for this project, so I rarely affected the overall beauty of the arrangement by removing a few flowers. I carried around a regular bound book, held tightly together with a rubber band, into which to slip these blossoms as soon as possible.

The resulting creation, bound with lace and ribbon, contained flowers from her wedding with notes about the symbolism of the blossoms. This kind of book is extremely versatile and does not necessarily have to revolve around a celebration (though it is a sweet idea for a fiftieth wedding anniversary, graduation, or birthday.) You can, for example, pick flowers from the woods, bind the project with calico, and send it to your hostess as a thank-you present for a weekend in the mountains.

The amount of time and trouble you go to is your decision. For a "quickie," simply take a photo album or small scrapbook and glue the flowers in place or cover them with clear self-adhesive film. Blank books, available in profusion at card shops and bookstores, also make good flower books.

The book shown here is a relatively complicated version. Each of the eight different flowers is captured between two pieces of clear plastic, and text accompanies each one. These are then bound with heavy paper covered with lace and tied with ribbon. It was a time-consuming project and falls into the category of a "love gift," one that is in no way time-effective but you don't really care because it is so special. There are many shorter, easier, less-expensive ways to do this. You can create these books for very little money in as short a time as two hours. But, like everything else, you get out what you put into it.

The most important aspect of this craft is that you are creating your own book with flowers that have special meaning or significance to you or to the lucky recipient of this gift. There is much symbolism and folklore associated with flowers, and the inclusion of a small amount of text with each entry will enhance the book. If your fancy runs to poetry, find an appropriate verse to go with each blossom.

TIME: 6–7 hours
LEAD TIME: A few weeks to press flowers
COST: ☆☆☆☆
MATERIALS:
    16 heavyweight cards, each 4½ × 6½ inches (approximately 11 × 16 cm). Available at stationery stores.
    Black photographic sleeves, 3½ × 5 inches (approximately

A

B

C

D

9 × 13 cm), with openings of 2¼ × 3 inches (approximately 6 × 8 cm). Available at art or photography stores.

X-Acto knife or razor blade
Pressed flowers
Craft glue
Black plastic or cloth tape
Hole punch
Card stock for cover
⅓ yard (30 cm) white cotton fabric
⅓ yard (30 cm) good-quality lace
1 yard (.9 m) 1¼-inch (3.6 cm) wide white satin ribbon
2 yards (1.8 m) ⅛-inch (.3 cm) wide white satin ribbon

DIFFICULTY: ✂ ✂ ✂ ✂+

SHELF LIFE: Should last a lifetime. Colors may fade over a period of years, but the flower forms will still be nice.

MAKING THE PAGES

1. Gather materials (photo A) and center a sleeve on a single card. Trace around the opening with a pencil, remove the sleeve, and cut out this opening with an X-Acto knife or safety razor blade (photo B).

2. Take the plastic out of the black sleeve and cut along two sides, opening it up fully.

3. Position pressed flowers as desired on the plastic. When you have them arranged, put a tiny spot of glue (Sobo or other craft glue that dries clear) underneath each flower and allow it to dry for a few minutes.

4. Replace the plastic inside the black sleeve. Trim if necessary, and tape each side of the sleeve with black plastic or cloth tape (photo C).

5. Place the sleeve, complete with flower, on the precut card, positioning the opening of the sleeve to match exactly the opening on the card, and glue in place.

6. Using a hole punch, make 3 evenly spaced holes along the left-hand side of the card. To make assembling the pages easier, be sure that the holes in each card line up with the others (photo D). Repeat for as many cards as you want to

include in the book. Note that after about 8 flower cards, the book tends to get a little too bulky.

7. Choose the text you want to go with each flower and write it on the cards, using a separate card for each different flower.

E

ASSEMBLING THE PAGES

Because the flowers are caught between clear plastic, you will need to put blank pages behind each floral page so the text won't show through. The flowers will be on the right-hand side, the text on the left, with blank pages in between.

> Page 1: Title page (*A Bride's Book of Flowers,* or *Sharon's Wedding Flowers,* or *Flowers from the Highlands,* or whatever is appropriate for your book)
> Page 2: Blank (reverse side of title page)
> Page 3: Blank
> Page 4: Text for flower one
> Page 5: Flower one
> Page 6: Blank
> Page 7: Blank
> Page 8: Text for flower two
> Page 9: Flower two, and so on

MAKING THE COVER AND BINDING

1. Cut a piece of card stock twice the width of your pages plus 3 inches (7.5 cm), and the length of the page plus 2 inches (5 cm). (The cover must completely surround the book on three sides and allow for a 1-inch [2.5 cm] margin on each side.)

2. Cut a piece of fabric and a piece of lace 2 inches (5 cm) wider and 3 inches (7.5 cm) longer than the card stock.

3. Glue the fabric to the card stock and the lace over the fabric, gluing the outside edges to the inside of the cover.

4. Cut two pieces of 1¼-inch (3.6-cm) wide ribbon 18 inches (45 cm) long. Glue one piece at the center just inside the front cover and the other piece at the center just inside the back cover. These will tie together to close the book.

ASSEMBLING THE BOOK

1. Take 8 inches (20 cm) of narrow ribbon and weave through the top holes of all the cards, being careful to keep the cards in order. Tie a knot to secure (photo E).

2. Repeat for the second and third holes.

3. Run a narrow ribbon 18 inches (45 cm) long through the loops of ribbon and down the outside spine of the book. Tie securely at the bottom to anchor the pages to the cover. *Note:* Don't tie so tightly that the pages will not turn easily.

Sample Texts

BLOODROOT: One of the first flowers to bloom in spring, bloodroot faces the hazards of a late frost. The leaves stay curled around the stem, protecting it from the cold, and unfurl only after the flower has been pollinated.

CARNATION: Carnations were once used to "combat melancholy and cheer the heart." A red carnation means admiration. A white means pure and ardent love and is a good-luck gift to a woman.

CHRISTMAS ROSE: The flower is considered a symbol of purity. This plant was said to have grown in the garden of heaven and was tended by the angels, who called it the rose of love.

CHRYSANTHEMUM: Chrysanthemum is a symbol of cheerfulness and optimism, of long life and happiness.

CROCUS: Symbol of youthful gladness, crocus is said to create merriment and cause much laughter. Crocus inspires romance and was often sent between lovers.

DAISY: A Dutch legend suggests that if you put daisies under your pillow, you will dream of your true love. Daisies are also used to tell the future of your love. Pluck the petals off one by one, chanting "he loves me" with the first, "he loves me not" with the next, and so on.

JOHNNY-JUMP-UP: The faces on these little flowers have inspired many common names such as tickle-my-fancy, kiss-her-in-the-pantry, and heartsease. These blossoms are said to cure a broken heart.

LILY OF THE VALLEY: If a newlywed couple plants lily of the valley together, their love will be renewed every spring when the plants bloom. Lily of the valley is also said to help humankind envision a better world.

NARCISSUS: "Let him who hath two loaves sell one, and buy the flower of narcissus, for bread is but food for the body, whereas narcissus is food for the soul."

PHLOX: Sweet-smelling phlox was often used in tussie-mussies or bouquets. According to the Victorian language of flowers, phlox portends a profession of love and a hope for sweet dreams.

PRIMROSE: The name *primrose* is thought to mean "most excellent." Fairies are said to take shelter under primrose leaves during a rainstorm. The German word for this flower means "little keys to heaven." (See photo E, page 37.)

SCILLA: The Welsh name for this plant is cuckoo's boots. A sixteenth-century botanist described it as "small blew flowers consisting of six little leaves spreade abrode like a star."

VERBENA: It was considered good luck for a bride to wear a garland of verbena blossoms she gathered herself. Scented water made from verbena blossoms, sprinkled in the dining room, will make guests merry. When tied with a yard of white satin ribbon, verbena blossoms bring a speedy recovery from sickness. Wearing verbena blossoms brings the gift of prophecy.

VINCA: Vinca, it was said, "induceth love between man and wife." The evergreen leaves have been chosen as a symbol of fidelity and friendship, while the blue blossoms represent the pleasure of happy memories. Planted outside the garden gate, vinca is an invitation to visit the garden.

Handmade Paper and Scented Ink

&

I am an enthusiastic letter writer, corresponding with many people throughout the country. Letters—those that I write and that I receive—have become very special to me, not only what they say but what they are written on. You can buy beautiful cards and lovely stationery, and can write with pens inked in every color of the rainbow, but if you really want to impress your correspondents, or if you want to give a very special gift to a pen pal, or any other kind of pal, then try handmade paper and a jar of scented ink. It is the ultimate in recycled paper.

Making paper is an ancient art practiced by the Egyptians over five thousand years ago. They split stems of papyrus plants, wove them together, beat them into flat sheets, and polished them with stones.

Luckily, the process today is greatly simplified, and made even easier and quicker with a few kitchen appliances such as a blender and microwave oven. You will also need to make or purchase the paper-making equipment called a mould and deckle, which can be found at art- and craft-supply stores, or at many nature or outdoor stores. The mould is a rectangular wooden box with a piece of screen or mesh stretched across the top. The deckle is the same size as the mould and rests on top of it. The pulp is caught on the mould before it is dried into paper.

It is difficult to get "paper thin" paper. Handmade paper is usually thick and heavy but has wonderful texture and can be truly beautiful with the addition of small leaves and petals, which are caught in the paper during the pressing stage.

For paper that you will want to write on, choose very light-colored petals and leaves. For paper that is to be a piece of art in itself, darker petals can also be used. If you use thick plant pieces they will not become embedded in the paper but can leave lovely impressions. Even though this does not add color, it can create beautiful effects.

TIME: 1 hour to make 5 sheets of paper

COST: ☆ (once you have the right equipment and if you recycle paper)

MATERIALS:

Scrap paper

Blender

Starch or sizing (optional)

Pan or sink full of water

Mould and deckle

Piece of screen

Sponge

Small leaves and petals (thin petals and leaves are the best to use: try blue phlox, honeysuckle, maidenhair fern, violets, Johnny-jump-up, pansy, spiderwort, rose, and impatiens)

Blotting paper
Rolling pin
Microwave oven
DIFFICULTY: ✂ ✂ ✂
SHELF LIFE: Indefinite

1. Tear scrap paper (photo A) into pieces approximately 1 inch (3 cm) square. Fill the blender about halfway with them. *Note:* The kind of paper you use to begin with greatly influences the kind of paper you end up with. The Sunday comics are colorful and will produce paper that looks like confetti. If your aim is to have the leaves and petals show up well on the finished paper, use white paper to begin with. Discarded computer paper works just fine. But remember, if you use cleaner paper, the resulting paper will be cleaner. If the waste paper has a lot of ink on it, your finished product will have a gray tinge.
2. Add about 6 inches (15 cm) of water.

A

B

3. Blend until the paper is dissolved and the pulp is fine and even. *Note:* The paper can be made stiffer at this point by adding 2 tablespoons of household starch to the pulp at this time. It can be made softer by adding a sizing, such as 1 tablespoon of flour or even oatmeal, which adds an interesting texture.
4. Fill a small plastic tub or sink until water stands at least 4–5 inches (10–13 cm) deep.
5. Submerge the mould and deckle in the water (photo B).
6. Pour the pulp into the water and swish the mould and deckle back and forth, catching the pulp within the frame. Continue until you have an even layer of pulp on top of the screen.
7. Lift the mould and deckle straight up out of the water, allowing the water to drain off, leaving the pulp flat on the screen.
8. Place the mould on a counter or table. Remove the deckle. You should have a thin layer of pulp on top of the screen at this point (photo C, page 41).
9. Place the extra piece of screen over the pulp. Use a sponge to remove as much water as possible from the fiber. Squeeze out the sponge and repeat the process.
10. Remove the mould, leaving the fiber on the loose piece of screen. You might have to peel it off the mould screen but it should come off fairly easily.
11. Add small pieces of leaves and petals at this stage. Sprinkle them at random over the page or make a small arrangement at the top or bottom. Remember to use very thin petals or leaves.
12. Put a piece of blotting paper on the counter on top of a small stack of newspaper. Turn the screen over so that the fiber sheet is between the screen and the blotting paper.
13. Using a rolling pin, roll the fiber sheet flat, removing excess water. This is called couching (photo D, page 41).
14. Couch again using a dry piece of blotting paper.
15. The fiber sheet should adhere to the blotting paper. Put both—blotting paper and fiber sheet—into the microwave

C

D

to dry for 2 minutes on high. Continue to dry in the microwave for 1 minute at a time until the sheet is dry. *Note:* Microwaves vary in intensity. Until you know exactly what your own oven will do, start slowly—no more than one minute on medium. Increase the intensity and time as necessary. If you don't have access to a microwave, allow the sheets to air-dry.

16. For a smooth, shiny finish, iron the paper with an iron set on low.

Scented Ink

Purchase or make floral water from roses or lemon balm. Add one teaspoon floral water to 2½ ounces (16 ml) of good-quality ink.

May Day Basket

My kitchen table has been submerged by a tidal wave of flowers and ribbons. Jars and bottles, pots and pans are filled to overflowing with bounty from the spring garden.

The making of May Day baskets is an annual event for my children and me. Each year we make a list of favorite friends and family members to whom we want to take baskets. Included in this list are people whom we may not know very well but who are a bit down on their luck and in need of a pick-me-up.

Giving May Day baskets is a charming European custom and one that should be adopted by more Americans. According to English tradition, the basket should be prepared the evening of the last day of April and delivered early on May 1. The most fun way to deliver the basket is to put it on the doorstep, ring the doorbell, and immediately run and hide, then secretly watch the look of happy surprise when a friend or loved one opens the door.

TIME: 30 minutes per basket
LEAD TIME: Some flowers should be conditioned overnight
COST: ☆ to ☆☆☆ (depending on basket)
MATERIALS:
    Fresh-cut flowers, such as azalea, daffodil, daisy, honeysuckle, lily, pansy, phlox, rose, snapdragon, tulip, wisteria
    Small jars (to fit down in the basket)
    Flat-bottomed basket
    Sphagnum moss
    Narrow ribbons to match flower colors
DIFFICULTY: ✂
SHELF LIFE: 3–14 days, depending on plant material used and how well it has been conditioned

A

B

6. Once the jars are filled, place bits of sphagnum moss in the basket to hide any sign of the glass jars.

Variation: Instead of using cut flowers, purchase small containers of bedding plants to put into the basket. This is a particularly welcome gift for a gardener, who can replant the flowers after enjoying the basket. Be sure to include planting and growing tips for each of the flowers included. (See the planting guide for flowers, pages 130–40.)

1. Condition the cut flowers properly (see Basic Techniques, page 123).
2. Weave ribbons through the handle or around the top of the basket. Tie bows at the sides or in front, and leave long tails (photo A).
3. Fill several jars three-quarters full of water and place them in the bottom of the basket.
4. Put the tallest branches or flowering stems into the center of the basket (photo B).
5. Keep adding flowers, gradually filling in the sides to make a triangular arrangement. Save the shortest blossoms for the front of the basket. If you have some "weeping" blossoms, such as wisteria, put them in the front to hang over the edge of the basket. The flowers can be grouped according to color or intermixed throughout. Be generous—you're giving away a taste of spring and you don't want to be miserly with it. Don't get frustrated if you have trouble "arranging" flowers. Just stick the stems in the jars of water. However you make it, every May Day basket has its own charm—just have fun.

Tussie-mussies

Mother's Day dawned clear and warm—a perfect spring day. The children got up early and fixed me their traditional Mother's Day breakfast of Cheerios and orange juice and then disappeared into the neighborhood to pursue their own adventures.

I was left in relative peace and solitude to prepare a Mother's Day package for my own mother. It was she who taught me my love of gardening, and so it was with particular pleasure that I wandered into the garden to give back some of the bounty that she has given me through the years.

Carefully I snipped choice flowers—a couple of perfect daisies, a small sprig of late yellow primrose, a purple and yellow viola, and a new white rosebud—and brought them inside to make a tussie-mussie for my mother.

Tussie-mussies are little bouquets of flowers caught up in bits of lace or paper doilies and ribbon. Along with sachets and nosegays, women of times past used these to help keep away disagreeable odors. In Victorian England, tussie-mussies took on a new meaning as each flower included in these miniature bouquets became symbolic of a different sentiment. Thus a tussie-mussie sent between two lovers might include a rose for love and success, a daisy for innocence, a primrose for young love, and phlox for sweet dreams.

The language of flowers is a fun way for friends and lovers to communicate. The symbolism of various flowers can be found in numerous books on flower folklore or the language of flowers.

COMMON FLOWERS AND THEIR SYMBOLISM

Aster: elegance; talisman of love
Bachelor's button: celibacy
Carnation (red): admiration
Carnation (white): pure and ardent love
Chrysanthemum (white): truth
Coreopsis: always cheerful
Daffodil: regard
Daisy: innocence, gentleness
Morning glory: farewell and departure
Pansy: thoughtful recollection
Peony: healing
Phlox: sweet dreams, profession of love

Fern: fascination
Forget-me-not: friendship
Geranium (scarlet): comfort
Hibiscus: delicate beauty
Hollyhock: ambition
Honesty: honest feelings
Impatiens: refusal
Iris: faith, wisdom, valor
Larkspur: open heart, ardent attachment
Lily of the valley: purity and humility
Rose (red): love and desire
Rose (yellow): jealousy
Rose (white): charm and innocence
Sunflower: devotion
Zinnia: thoughts of absent friends

TIME: **15 minutes**

COST: ☆

MATERIALS:
Fresh flowers
Paper doily or inexpensive lace (or even expensive lace if your budget allows)
Florist's tape
1 yard (1 m) ½-inch (1-cm) wide ribbon

DIFFICULTY: ✂

SHELF LIFE: Out of water, it should last 6–7 hours. If the stems are unwrapped and placed in a small glass of water, the tussie-mussie should last several days.

1. Gather and condition the desired flowers (photo A; see Basic Techniques, page 123).
2. Choose a large central flower that represents the essence of the message you want to send (a rose or large daisy, for example).
3. Place a ring of interesting, scented foliage around the central flower.
4. Place a ring of smaller flowers around the foliage and keep building concentric circles of plants until you are pleased with the arrangement.
5. Wrap a damp paper towel around the stem and place a piece of plastic wrap around the paper towel.
6. Cut an X in the center of a paper doily or a circle of lace and put the wrapped stems through this cut.
7. Wrap the stems with floral tape, catching the center of the doily in the tape to give it a pleated look.
8. Spiral ribbon up the stems, make a bow at the top, and leave long tails (photo B). You may want to add another bow between the flowers and the lace.

A

B

Rosebud Napkin Ring

❧

Spring is a glorious time of year to entertain. My garden is usually filled with enough flowers to make me feel generous and a May luncheon for a half-dozen favorite lady friends is the perfect time and place to share my springtime bounty.

The place settings at the table can double as party favors for all the guests. Rosebud napkin rings, tiny wicker wheelbarrows full of potted herbs, and place cards decorated with dried flowers all combine to create a truly beautiful table. When your guests leave after the party, let them take these home as lovely mementos of a pleasant spring day.

A

B

TIME: 30 minutes

LEAD TIME: 3 weeks to dry rosebuds

COST: ☆

MATERIALS:
  Small heart-shaped picture frame
  6–8 tiny dried rosebuds
  Glue gun
  Wooden curtain ring 2 inches (5 cm) across
  White floral tape

DIFFICULTY: ✂ ✂

SHELF LIFE: Indefinite (rosebuds may fade after a year or so)

1. Take apart picture frame, keeping only the heart-shaped front.
2. Using the glue gun, glue the rosebuds in place on the frame (photo A).
3. Wrap the wooden ring with the white floral tape, covering it well.
4. Glue the back of the frame to the ring at a 45-degree angle so that it will stand up by itself (photo B).
5. To showcase the roses, slip a napkin through the ring.

Pressed-Flower Place Cards

❧

TIME: 5 minutes per card

LEAD TIME: Several days to press and dry flowers

COST: ☆

MATERIALS:
  3 × 6-inch (8 × 16-cm) cards
  Pressed flowers
  Clear self-adhesive film

DIFFICULTY: ✂

SHELF LIFE: Indefinite

1. Fold the cards in half lengthwise to make them stand up.
2. Write a guest's name on the front half of each card, leaving enough room for a flower.

with each division. If you are still counting leaves on your own plants, purchase containers of herbs that you can divide, and put these into small baskets. Guests can take home the rooted herbs to plant in their own gardens, a lasting reminder of the good times had that day.

Some of the best herbs to use for this project include thyme, lemon balm, oregano, marjoram, chives, and mint. Or use whatever you have an excess of in your garden. If you really want to make it special—and useful—include an instruction card to go with each herb, telling how to care for it in the garden. (See planting guide for herbs, pages 140–43.)

3. Place a small pressed flower on the card, making sure that you can still read the name easily.
4. Cut a piece of clear self-adhesive film slightly larger than the card. Peel off the backing and place the film over the card, securing the flower to the card. Be careful to keep the flower in the same place on the card. Sometimes the sticky film acts like a magnet and the flower will jump up to it before you're ready. Practice with a mediocre flower to begin with, saving the best flowers for the real thing.

Variation: This technique can also be used to make very attractive note cards and stationery.

TIME: 5 minutes per basket
COST: ☆
MATERIALS:
    Wheelbarrow or other novelty basket
    Rooted herbs
DIFFICULTY: ✂
SHELF LIFE: 2–3 days

1. Line small baskets with pieces of black or dark green plastic.
2. Fill the baskets with potting soil.
3. Plant rooted herbs and water carefully. Be sure that the baskets of herbs are not dripping water *at all* before you put them on your good tablecloth.

Wheelbarrow Basket of Herbs

&

You can sometimes find small baskets made into the shape of wheelbarrows or carts, and these look charming with bits of rooted herbs in them. If you can't find these shapes, use any small basket. If your herbs are big enough to share, dig them from your own garden, making sure to gather plenty of roots

Dollhouse Garden

✂

My goddaughter is a child of doting parents and even more doting grandparents. This child lacks nothing, making it quite a challenge for me to come up with a gift for her on her birthday.

Like many little girls, she loves playing with miniatures, so it occurred to me that perhaps she would like a miniature yard to go along with her dollhouse.

The result far surpassed my expectations. I grew a flat of grass and gave her a bag of modeling clay, some dollhouse lawn furniture, some pebbles, a small bag full of dried flowers, and a pair of small scissors and told her to use her imagination.

She loved it. She carefully and happily cut the grass often with the scissors. She made pebble paths and then created a birdbath—complete with bird—made from the modeling clay. When I last saw her she was creating flower beds with the dried flowers and making a swing set from the clay.

It was a perfect gift for her because it challenged her imagination and left plenty of room for her creativity. The grass is fairly easy to grow, even indoors, with regular watering and enough sunshine. When this flat of grass finally dies out, it will be just as much fun for her to start all over again, "tilling" the soil and planting the grass herself.

TIME: **30 minutes**

LEAD TIME: **3 weeks from dirt to grass garden**

COST: ☆ to ☆☆ (depending on container; accessories will be extra)

MATERIALS:

　Basket, tray, or clear plastic box about 15 × 18 inches (38 × 45 cm), at least 5–6 inches (13–15 cm) deep (I used a plastic sweater box)

　Black plastic garbage bag (to line basket)

　Cup of small pebbles

　6–8 cups (1.5–2 liters) potting soil

⅛ pound (57 g) rye grass seed

　Any desired accessories (modeling clay, miniature furniture, birdhouses, and so on)

DIFFICULTY: ✂

SHELF LIFE: Grass should last a couple of months if it gets sufficient sunlight and water and is treated to a weak fertilizer solution once a month.

1. If you are using a basket, cut a piece of black plastic garbage bag large enough to line the bottom and sides of the basket.
2. Place pebbles in the bottom of the container at least 1 inch (3 cm) deep (photo A).
3. Fill the container with potting soil.
4. Generously sprinkle grass seed over the top of the soil and cover with a very thin layer of potting soil.
5. Water well and keep evenly moist. Place in a sunny window. Grass should germinate in a couple of days and should be 2–3 inches (5–8 cm) tall within 2 weeks (photo B).

A

B

C

6. The possibilities are endless in this miniature landscape (photo C). Make small moss-covered hills. Plant a tiny tree. Create a hedge of tiny plants. Stick in dried flower blossoms for an instant flower garden, or root very small live flowers. Display a small bonsai tree, add dollhouse lawn furniture, make pebble walks, or even create a garden pond. You are restricted only by your imagination. Many women play with their daughters' dollhouses more than the daughters do, and this may be true of these miniature landscapes as well.

Easter Egg Hunt Centerpiece

&

The miniature garden detailed in the Dollhouse Garden project can also be used to create an incomparable centerpiece for a dinner party. For an Easter buffet, try creating a miniature Easter egg hunt for the center of your table (see page 2).

See the preceding project for full instructions on making the miniature garden that forms the basis of this centerpiece. Use an interesting basket, making sure to line the bottom and sides of the basket with black plastic first. Start at least three weeks before you'll need this for your Easter Sunday brunch. Add tiny colored eggs (available at many craft stores) or use real quail eggs—they are just the right size. Tiny baskets of dried flowers and ribbons and a small clay rabbit add a colorful touch to this conversation piece.

Two huge mimosa trees stood guard over my childhood home, their branches intertwining over the rooftop. They were magical trees and I often climbed their thick, spreading branches to escape into the world of the sky and to watch the world below me. ℰ It was high in these trees that I learned one of those important lessons in life. I had climbed higher than usual one day and suddenly got scared. I called for my father to help me down and he ambled over, peered up into the tree, and said, "You got yourself up there, looks like you can get yourself down." And he sat down to wait. Although I was incensed by his attitude, he was right: the short little legs that got me up there also got me down. ℰ While climbing was exciting, it was the glorious pink puffball blossoms that I loved

Summer Bounty

best about the mimosa trees. I would pick these delicate, sweet-smelling flowers and use them as play makeup. These blossoms inspired me later to search out plants that would soothe the skin, help the complexion, or offer a lingering sweet scent. ℰ The world of natural beauty products is not only exciting but is becoming more and more important commercially. The bounty from your garden can give you the basic ingredients for making sweetly scented soaps, perfumes, and bath oils. Just the right combination of herbs and flowers will allow you to make bath bags and ointments to soothe, stimulate, or heal. ℰ Make a basket of beauty products in the summertime and give them away for birthdays, hostess gifts, or just little love gifts. Take a friend a basket of bath bags good for soothing furrowed brows—she'll thank you profusely.

Bath Bags

&

The women I know spend a tremendous amount of energy doing the things they do. Whether we spend our time training for a triathlon, doing management training, or toilet training a toddler, most of us end our days tired and draggy. I've found that a perfect end-of-the-day treat is a long bath scented with a special bath bag or a drop or two of bath oil.

Through the ages, folk healers have known that different herbs produce different results in the bath. Some herbs will soothe while others stimulate. Some are good for reducing stress while others seem to be effective in revitalizing aching muscles. Lavender, which is sweetly scented and seems to cure a variety of ills, can be included in almost any bath bag. You can add the herbs directly to the bath water, but this is rather messy since the herbs will stick to your skin and may clog the drain. A much more pleasant way to take an herbal bath is to make a bath bag, essentially an oversized tea bag that puts the herbal essence into the bath water without all the mess. Adding a small amount of oatmeal or powdered milk to each bath bag will help soften the skin.

Choose combinations of herbs to cure whatever ails you and make bundles of bags for yourself and to give to friends. See the list following the project instructions for herb suggestions.

TIME: 30 minutes for 10 bags

COST: ☆

MATERIALS:

 12 × 6-inch (30 × 15-cm) strips of muslin, cheesecloth, or calico

 Needle and thread or sewing machine

 Dried herbs

 Oatmeal or powdered milk

 String or ribbon

 Tags for identification

DIFFICULTY: ✂

SHELF LIFE: 1 year or more

1. Fold fabric strips in half, right sides together, and sew along the two long sides. Turn bag right side out.
2. Mix a selection of dried herbs, choosing a certain "theme" for each mixture (soothing, stimulating, and so on). Add 1 cup (250 ml) oatmeal or powdered milk for every four cups (1 liter) of dried herbs. This amount will make ten bath bags.
3. Put ½ cup (125 ml) of herb-oatmeal mixture in a prepared bag. Tie securely with a long loop of string or ribbon so the bag can be hung from the faucet into the water.
4. Include an identifying tag explaining the mixture's theme.

SOOTHING HERBS: Catnip · Chamomile flowers · Comfrey · Evening primrose flowers · Jasmine flowers · Juniper berries · Lemon balm · Lime flowers · Mullein leaves or flowers • Rose flowers • Rose geranium leaves • Violet leaves or flowers

STIMULATING HERBS: Basil • Bay • Calendula flowers • Lavender • Marjoram • Mint • Pine needles • Rosemary • Sage • Thyme

HERBS FOR ACHING MUSCLES: Bay • Juniper berries • Oregano • Poplar buds and bark • Sage • Strawberry leaves

HERBS TO REDUCE STRESS: Bee balm • Lemon balm • Lavender • Rose

Bath Oils

&

A few drops of sweetly scented oil transform the bath from a necessity into an indulgent luxury. If you're taking a bath to get clean as well as to relax, wait until you've been in the tub for about ten minutes and then add the oil. The oil coats your skin and keeps water from penetrating. Be careful getting in and out of the tub, because the oil will make it slippery.

TIME: 10 minutes

COST: ☆ to ☆☆

MATERIALS:

 1 tablespoon herbal essential oils (lavender, rose, jasmine, sandalwood)

 4 tablespoons almond oil

 1 tablespoon vodka or undenatured alcohol

 Small glass or plastic bottles

DIFFICULTY: ✂

SHELF LIFE: Indefinite

1. Mix the ingredients in a glass jar with screw-on lid.
2. Pour into small decorative jars and label. This mixture makes 3 ounces (90 ml).

Variations: Massage oil can be made the same way, without the vodka. Use the list of herbs given above to create the kind of massage oil wanted (such as lavender for soothing or rosemary for stimulating). For herbal skin oil, add one tablespoon ground rosemary or sage to four ounces (120 ml) almond oil to make a skin ointment that cleanses and moisturizes. Keep it in the refrigerator.

Herbal Vinegars

&

My friend Ann is a wonderful cook and, like many good cooks today, is conscientious about cutting down on the amount of fat she serves. She often uses flavored vinegars on salads, in marinades, as a substitute for lemon or lime juice, or to flavor cooked vegetables.

Herbal vinegars make lovely and useful gifts. The vinegars can be spiced up with many different combinations of herbs to add a variety of flavors to salad dressings and sauces. Some of the best combinations of herbs include sage and parsley; coriander and basil; tarragon, basil, chives, and garlic; and thyme, dill seed, and dill leaf.

There are many different kinds of vinegars available. Some of the best are rice, white wine, champagne, sherry, cider, and fruit vinegars. The least desirable and the least expensive is distilled white vinegar, which tends to have a sharp taste.

Vinegars can be stored in many different kinds of containers, including interesting glass jars, recycled wine bottles, or oil jars. Be on the lookout for unusual bottles. You can often pick up inexpensive ones at flea markets. Use corks rather than metal lids, which corrode quickly from the acidity of the vinegar. Hardware stores generally have corks to fit odd-sized bottles.

A

Flavoring vinegar is a simple process, and one that can result in a bottle for the pantry shelf that is beautiful as well as useful.

TIME: 20 minutes
LEAD TIME: 2–3 weeks to steep
COST: ☆
MATERIALS:
    Herbs
    Glass container with noncorrosive lid
    Good-quality vinegar, such as rice or white wine
DIFFICULTY: ✄
SHELF LIFE: Up to a year or more if stored properly

1. Gather herbs (photo A) and place in the bottom of a glass container. To get the most flavor, use chopped herbs at a rate of ⅓–½ cup (80–125 ml) of fresh or ¼ cup (60 ml) of dried herbs per quart (1 liter) of vinegar.
2. Fill jar with vinegar.
3. Allow to steep in a sunny window for 2–3 weeks.
4. Strain the herbs from the vinegar. Add a fresh sprig or two of herbs, if desired. For an elegant presentation, tie a ribbon around the neck of the bottle, and include a small bunch of dried flowers with spring and summer gifts or bells and greenery at Christmastime.

Dried Herbs
❧

Spices and herbs from the grocery store can be very expensive. The bounty from the herb garden is such that you can package up and dry herbs by the bundle to share with your friends. You can, of course, hand your friend a collection of paper bags with a different dried herb in each bag, but it makes a much more exciting gift to buy small, inexpensive glass jars for each herb and put them in a small herb rack.

The herbs can be air dried or dried in the microwave, depending on your resources, time restraints, and the kinds of herbs you are drying. Another alternative is to cover a cookie sheet with stems of herbs and put it in a barely warm conventional oven. After about 20 minutes the herbs should be crisp and ready to package.

Do not store herbs in an airtight container until they are thoroughly dry.

Rose Perfume
❧

As I worked in my garden one morning, a sudden breeze mixed the fragrances of the flowers and brought them close to me. It was such a delightful odor that I wanted to capture it somehow, to hold it in my hand. But since a scent is a fleeting thing, it became diluted when the breeze died and the sun beat down on the flowers. To drink in their fragrance I had to go closer.

The desire to capture the fragrance of flowers is an ancient one and has resulted in perfumes and cosmetics that are worth more than gold. Today a floral scent is often created synthetically to reduce the cost of these products, but synthetic scents will never completely match the glory of a fully opened scented rose.

Although it is difficult to create a really fine perfume at home without the proper equipment, it is easy to make up

your own perfumes, skin toners, and soaps with a few basic ingredients. Bottle it, name it, label it, and give it to your favorite friends. They'll think of you and your garden every time they use it.

TIME: **30 minutes**
LEAD TIME: **3–4 weeks maturation**
COST: ☆ to ☆☆
MATERIALS:
    ¼ cup (60 ml) rose water
    2 tablespoons rose oil
    1 tablespoon rosemary oil
    1 tablespoon storax oil
    1 cup (250 ml) vodka or undenatured alcohol

1. Mix ingredients together in a glass jar with lid.
2. Allow mixture to mature for 3–4 weeks, shaking often to mix scents.
3. Pour carefully into small atomizers or bottles.

Rose Soap

&

I know that it's not exactly the same thing, but the next time you have a midnight urge to go into the kitchen to make something, try making soap instead of fudge. It's much better for you, and cleanup is a snap!

Real soap making is a long, hot, involved process, but this easy version only takes an hour or so. By melting down hard, pure soap, adding essential oils, and pouring it into molds, you can make your own soaps.

TIME: **1 hour**
COST: ☆ (for 12–24 small soap pieces)

MATERIALS:
    Molds (try candy molds, which come in a variety of interesting shapes and sizes)
    Vaseline
    2 4-ounce (100 g) bars glycerine or castile soap
    Food processor or metal grater
    Enamel saucepan
    Rose water
    Rose oil
DIFFICULTY: ✄ ✄ ✄
SHELF LIFE: Indefinite (the harder the soap, the longer it will last)

1. Grease the molds with a small amount of Vaseline.
2. Grate the soap in a food processor or with a metal grater.
3. Put the soap flakes in an enamel saucepan, add 2 tablespoons of rose water and 10 drops of rose oil, and heat slowly.
4. Stir until soap has melted and is the consistency of whipped cream.
5. Remove from heat and quickly put a small amount of mixture into each mold. Use your hands to press the "dough" firmly into the molds, making sure that there are no air pockets.
6. Allow the soap to harden overnight in the molds. Remove them and place on a tray to harden further.

Lavender Vinegar
&

Vinegars are usually used in the kitchen for cooking or flavoring, but they are also useful as cosmetic toners and astringents. Floral vinegars, diluted with clear spring water, can be used daily to improve the texture of the skin. This lavender vinegar is not only good for your skin but is also a beautiful rosy purple color and looks pretty in a jar on your dressing table.

TIME: 10 minutes
LEAD TIME: 2–3 days maturation
COST: ☆
MATERIALS:
    ¼ cup (60 ml) fresh or dried lavender
    ¼ cup (60 ml) fresh mint leaves
    1½ cups (375 ml) cider vinegar
    Spring water
DIFFICULTY: ✂
SHELF LIFE: Indefinite

1. Mix together the lavender, mint, and vinegar and place in a clear glass jar.

2. Cover the jar and place in sun for 2–3 days until color from lavender has transferred to liquid.
3. Strain out the herbs.
4. Dilute by mixing ½ cup (125 ml) floral vinegar with 2 cups (500 ml) spring water.

Summer Fare
&

When going to a friend's mountain house for the Fourth of July weekend, I wanted to take something to my hostess that would be pretty and practical. I finally decided on a long-lasting picnic in a basket: salsa, pesto sauce, and a jar of herbs for tea, all made from the bounty of my garden. The salsa will probably be put out with chips immediately upon our arrival. The pesto, I suspect, will be a welcome instant pasta topping for family supper after all the guests have left.

Salsa

TIME: 1 hour
COST: ☆ (if you use all homegrown ingredients)
MATERIALS:
    1 cup (250 ml) chopped tomatoes
    ½ cup (125 ml) diced peppers (poblano, bell, jalapeño—whatever you like)
    2 tablespoons finely chopped onion
    2 cloves finely chopped garlic
    2 tablespoons lemon juice or flavored vinegar (tarragon is excellent)
    1 tablespoon olive oil (can be flavored with basil, garlic, or peppers)
    2 teaspoons fresh rosemary
    ½ teaspoon salt

½ teaspoon sugar
Ground pepper to taste
DIFFICULTY: ✂ ✂
SHELF LIFE: 1 week (refrigerated)

Combine all ingredients and place in a glass jar or container. Refrigerate for at least 1 hour to blend the flavors. Makes 2 pints (1 liter). To make a pretty gift, tie a bundle of small dried red peppers together with green ribbon and tie around the top of the jar.

Pesto Sauce

TIME: 30 minutes
COST: ☆
MATERIALS:
   1½ cups (375 ml) fresh basil
   ½ cup (125 ml) parsley or seasoning celery leaves
   ½ cup (125 ml) olive oil
   ¼ cup (60 ml) pine nuts
   3 cloves garlic
   ½ cup (125 ml) grated Parmesan cheese
DIFFICULTY: ✂
SHELF LIFE: 1 week (refrigerated)

1. Place torn basil leaves, parsley, olive oil, pine nuts, and garlic in a food processor and process until well blended.
2. Place in a glass jar or container and store in the refrigerator. Add Parmesan cheese just before serving. Makes 1 cup

(250 ml). If giving as a gift, place the Parmesan cheese in a small plastic bag and use a colorful ribbon to tie the cheese and a sprig of basil to the top of the jar.

Herbal Tea

Bees and butterflies create waves of soft, silent colors in my garden. With their large, silky wings, butterflies seem to be creatures almost too lovely to be real. They flock around the lantana or the bee balm, sometimes taking turns, sometimes congregating as if at a tea party. Perhaps it was because the bees and butterflies found bee balm so delicious that Indians and pioneers decided to try it for themselves. Whatever the reason, the leaves of this native plant have been used for centuries to make a delicious herbal tea.

Tea can be made from many herbs grown in your garden and makes a wonderful gift. Create a basket of herbal teas for a special friend and include a tea for every need—catnip to induce sleep, bee balm for a refreshing summer iced drink, chamomile for restless children, and mint to soothe an upset stomach.

The best way to give herbal teas as gifts is to dry the leaves and put them in a small jar. Include a tea strainer or a pretty mug in the basket to complete the gift.

The following herbs make very good teas: bee balm (leaves and flowers) · blackberry (leaves) · catnip (leaves) · chamomile (flowers) · hibiscus (flowers) · jasmine (flowers) *(Caution: Do not use Carolina jasmine, which is poisonous.)* · mint (leaves) · rose hips

1. Pour 1 cup (250 ml) of boiling water over fresh or dried leaves or flowers. A general rule of thumb is 1 tablespoon fresh or 2 teaspoons dried herbs per cup of water.
2. Let the herbs steep from a few minutes to a half hour, depending on personal taste.
3. Flavor with honey, if desired.

Variation: To make iced tea, prepare hot tea and then cool it in the refrigerator.

Baby Basket

&

When Linda's baby girl was born, I thought of bringing her flowers, of course, but I really wanted to take something that would last longer than just a few days.

A quick trip to the craft store and a toy store resulted in a cute little wicker rickshaw and a pink bunny. I filled the vehicle with dried pink flowers and arranged the bunny to look as if it pulled the basket. With pleasure, I took the gift to Linda and the baby. If it is handled carefully, it should last for years.

TIME: **30 minutes**
COST: ☆ to ☆☆☆

MATERIALS:
Dried flowers (for a traditional look, use pink for a girl, yellow and blue for a boy)
Basket (wheelbarrow or rickshaw if you can find it)
Ribbon
Small stuffed animal
DIFFICULTY: ✄
SHELF LIFE: Indefinite

1. Cut the stems so that the dried flowers will just peek above the top of the basket.
2. Begin filling the basket at the sides and gradually work your way into the center. The center should be a little fuller and taller than the edges. Arrange the flowers as if they were bundles in a flower cart at the market. Decorate the basket with ribbon.
3. Have the stuffed animal "pull" or hold the basket.

Flavored Cooking Oils

&

We recently visited a wonderful restaurant where we had a memorable meal. As soon as we sat down, the waiter magically appeared with a basket full of warm bread and two cruets of flavored oils into which to dip the bread. It is, perhaps, not the healthiest, but it is certainly one of the most delicious ways to eat hard, crusty bread.

Inspired by this treat, I decided to make my own oils. I found that flavoring the oils is easy. The trick is to use a high-quality olive oil as well as fresh herbs or peppers. This makes a good hostess gift, since it can be opened and used immediately or saved for later. Even if your hostess never opens it, the jars packed with peppers and garlic look beautiful on the shelf.

TIME: 20 minutes

COST: ☆ to ☆☆

MATERIALS:

    Mustard seeds

    Whole black peppercorns

    One-pint (500-ml) glass jars

    Peppers (poblano, Scotch bonnets, jalapeño, or the like; or use bell peppers if you prefer a milder taste)

    Whole garlic cloves, peeled

    Extra virgin olive oil

    Basil sprigs

DIFFICULTY: ✂ ✂

SHELF LIFE: Several months

Pepper Oil

The heat from the peppers is quickly transferred to the oil, but a jar packed full of different kinds of peppers is so attractive on the shelf, you may choose to leave the peppers in the oil rather than remove them to cook with the oil. Depending on the kind of peppers used, this oil may have a fairly hot bite to it.

1. Place mustard seeds and black peppercorns in the bottom of the jars.

2. Pack peppers and garlic on top of the spices, filling the jar. Carefully pour olive oil into the jar until it is filled to within ¼ inch (.5 cm) of the top.

3. If you like, you can process the jars by placing them in boiling water for 15 minutes. (See Basic Techniques, page 126.)

Basil or Garlic Oil

Place 6–8 peeled garlic cloves *or* 4–6 sprigs of basil in the bottom of a glass container and fill with olive oil. After 2 weeks, strain the oil to remove the herbs. Use with vinegar for salad dressings, or for dipping with bread. Don't leave the herbs in too long or the oil may develop mold.

Woven Herb Basket

&

An excess of thyme and a cute little basket made of wood and chicken wire prompted me to create a woven basket to take to a friend who is moving into a new house. She loves baskets and has a nice collection of them in her new country kitchen. A variety of herbs can be woven through the chicken wire, transforming the basket into a fragrant work of art. Choose any herbs with long, supple stems—whatever is abundant in your own garden—but thyme is especially wonderful, because the leaves are so small and it dries so nicely. Besides, what could be more useful to a harried housewife than a basket of thyme?

TIME: 1 hour

COST: ☆ to ☆☆

MATERIALS:

    Honeysuckle or wild grape vine

    Small chicken-wire basket, 10 × 5 × 4 inches (25 × 13 × 10 cm)

Plastic vegetable bag half full of long strands of fresh
  herbs (thyme, oregano, lavender, mint)
Wire or string
Sturdy floral wire 18 inches (45 cm) long
DIFFICULTY: ✄ ✄ ✄
SHELF LIFE: Indefinite

A

1. Wrap long pieces of vine around the top of the basket,
   securing with wire or string (photo A). Then, beginning at
   the bottom of the basket at one side, take several strands
   of herbs together and weave the stems in and out of the
   holes in the chicken wire along the bottom of the basket
   (photo B). Be careful not to strip the leaves off the stems
   as you pull them through. It is not necessary to go in and
   out of every hole—skip one or two periodically.
2. When you have woven the first set of stems, take several
   more long stems and begin weaving again, in the next set

B

of holes up. Do not start them directly above where the others were started. It will give a smoother finish if you stag-
ger the starting points.
3. Continue weaving the stems through the holes in rows until
   the entire basket is covered.
4. Take the floral wire and several stems full of leaves and
   weave over and under the wire, securing the stems at the
   ends of the wire.
5. Curve this gently to form a handle and firmly secure the
   ends of the wire to opposite sides of the basket.

Bouquet Garni

Trimming the herb garden always leaves me with handfuls of
leaves and snippets of stems from my favorite herbs. These are

perfect to dry and combine to make small herbal flavoring bags called *bouquet garni.* Caught in a small ball of cheesecloth, the dried herbs are perfect for flavoring soup or adding to a pot of simmering stew or stewing chicken. This kiss of seasoning lends a subtle blend of flavors to enhance many dishes.

As a great gift for a cook, place several of these small bags in a basket or glass jar.

TIME: 30 minutes for 18 small bags

COST: ☆

MATERIALS:

½ yard (45 cm) 9-inch (23-cm) wide double-strength cheesecloth

¼ cup (60 ml) ground marjoram

¼ cup (60 ml) dried thyme leaves

¼ cup (60 ml) dried parsley leaves

¼ cup (60 ml) dried rosemary leaves

1 tablespoon ground sage

1 tablespoon crumbled bay leaf

1 tablespoon oregano

Cotton string

DIFFICULTY: ✂ ✂

SHELF LIFE: Indefinite

1. Cut 18 2-inch (5-cm) squares from the cheesecloth (photo A).
2. Mix herbs together and divide the mixture evenly among the cheesecloth squares.
3. Tie into small balls and secure with a long piece of cotton

A

string. To use, drop a bag into a pot during cooking and remove before serving.

Garden in a Box

&

Many stores and catalogs sell a garden in a box—dried flowers placed in a printer's tray, with each compartment holding a different type of flower. These wooden trays, originally used to hold metal type, have been popular for years for displaying miniatures.

Even though stores charge a fortune for them, the box garden concept is simple. Fill each of the compartments with a different kind of dried flower and arrange them so that the entire box looks like a miniature landscape. This kind of garden has a lot of advantages. It is portable, never needs watering, and never has weeds!

TIME: 1–1½ hours
COST: ☆ to ☆☆
MATERIALS:
    1 12-inch (30-cm) square "printer's tray" divided into several compartments (available at craft stores)
    Dried flowers
    Glue gun
DIFFICULTY: ✂ ✂
SHELF LIFE: Indefinite (flower colors may fade after a year or so)

1. Lay out flowers in the box's compartments, alternating light and dark, bright and soft colors (photo A).
2. When you are satisfied with the arrangement, glue the flowers to the box. You may want the flowers to appear in neat rows, or you may prefer a more casual arrangement. Begin by gluing rows of flowers to the perimeter of each section. Then fill in each compartment with the same kind of flowers, gluing the flowers to each other in the center of the compartments.

A

Herb Box

A nice variation on the garden in a box is the herb box, a small wooden box with compartments above and pegs for hanging dried herbs underneath. It makes a lovely wall hanging for the kitchen, a sort of indoor herb garden.

TIME: 1–1½ hours
COST: ☆ to ☆☆
MATERIALS:
    Dried herbs
    Wooden box with pegs and compartments (available at craft stores)
    Paint or markers for writing on wood
    Glass or Plexiglas to fit over compartments
DIFFICULTY: ✂ ✂
SHELF LIFE: Indefinite

1. Choose the herbs you want to include and make small bundles of each.
2. Write the name of each herb under a separate compartment.
3. Place choice sprigs of each herb in the designated compartment (photo A).
4. Hang a small bunch of herbs from each peg.
5. Using a suitable adhesive, attach the glass or Plexiglas over the compartments.

A

Pot of Larkspur

&

Pots of dried flowers and "garden walls" made from rows of dried flowers are very popular—and very expensive in stores. Yet they can be made easily and are inexpensive if you dry your own flowers. Even if you have to purchase the flowers already dried, they are still very reasonable.

TIME: **30 minutes**
COST: ☆ (not including flowers)
MATERIALS:
    Small clay pot, 8 × 3 × 4 inches (20 × 8 × 10 cm)
    Florist's oasis
    2 dozen stalks of pink larkspur
    Sheet moss
    1½ yards (1.5 m) 2-inch (5-cm) wide wire-edged ribbon
DIFFICULTY: ✂ ✂
SHELF LIFE: Indefinite

1. Cut oasis to fit the bottom of the clay pot (photo A), wedging it in so that it is very secure.
2. Arrange stalks of larkspur until it looks pleasing to you, pushing the stalks all the way into the dry oasis (photo B).
3. Use the moss to cover the top of the oasis. Allow tiny strands to creep over the edge of the pot.

B

A

4. Tie the ribbon around most of the stalks, allowing a few to stand free outside. This will keep the arrangement from looking strangled. Tie a bow on one side.

Naturally Dyed Cloth

&

The bright colors of my late-summer garden seem to be crying out to be used for something. There is perhaps no lovelier way to capture the bounty of the garden than to dye cloth or yarn. Colors produced from garden plants and flowers are soft and subtle and completely different from those produced by synthetic dyes. Sometimes the original colors will fool you. Bright purple onions, for example, make a lovely light brown dye. Naturally, you will use the plant materials that are most available to you, and you will create the colors you like best.

Silk, cotton, and wool that have not been treated with any kind of chemical will take dye best. Wash the fabric or yarn first to make sure that it is clean and will take the color easily. Synthetics generally do not dye well.

If you want to create a long-lasting product that you can wash without disturbing the color, you must use a chemical called a mordant to make the colors stay. Natural dyeing can be a very detailed and complicated process that takes days to do properly. The directions here are for "quick dyeing," that is, without a mordant, and are given for fun—to get cloth or wool that is beautifully dyed, but also to experiment with colors from your garden. The colors will be lovely, but you *cannot* wash the material because the dye will not be set. Granted, this greatly lessens the usefulness of the dyed cloth, but if you are making something that doesn't need to be washed (for example, small bags for potpourri or a wall hanging of some sort) or if you are working with children and want a quick craft, don't worry about the mordants. Just have fun with it.

Once I used an old pot that had a rusty spot on the bottom, thinking that would be like adding iron as a mordant, but it didn't quite work out that way. The cloth rested on the bottom of the pan for fifteen or twenty minutes at one point, and the rust stained the fabric. This could have been avoided by using an enamel pot or at least one that was not rusty, or by not allowing the cloth to sit in one spot for so long.

I used four different plants and dyed small amounts from each one. I cut the fabric into 8-inch (20 cm) squares and sewed these together to make a throw for the guest bedroom.

PLANT	DYE COLOR
Aster (purple flower)	Yellow green
Bloodroot (root)	Orange
Calliopsis	Red orange
Dahlia (red)	Orange
Gaillardia	Light gold
Goldenrod (flower)	Yellowish tan
Hollyhock (red)	Orange
Iris (purple flower)	Blue violet
Lily of the valley (leaf)	Green
Marigold	Yellow
Onion (purple skins)	Light brown
Zinnia (yellow)	Bright yellow

TIME: 2–3 hours, though some plants must soak overnight
COST: ☆ to ☆☆☆ (depending on choice of fabric)
MATERIALS:
  Appropriate plant material
  Silk, cotton, or wool fabric or yarn
  Soap and water
DIFFICULTY: ✂ ✂ ✂ ✂
SHELF LIFE: Indefinite (if not washed)

1. Chop up any roots or woody stems and cover with clear water. Let soak overnight. Leaves and blossoms should soak at least 2 hours. Berries should soak 30 minutes.
2. Hand wash fabric or yarn with a mild soap and rinse well.
3. Put plant material in a large enamel pan (photo A) and cover with water. Bring to a boil, then turn down heat to simmer for 1½–2 hours.
4. Strain out plant material and put dye bath back into pan.
5. Add *wet* cloth or yarn to dye bath.
6. Simmer until desired color is obtained (photo B), anywhere from 10 minutes to 2 hours. Stir cloth frequently.

A

B

Perhaps of all the seasons, fall brings back the sweetest memories of growing up. Autumn was a time for the pungent smell of muscadines in our local woods, and a time for kicking crisp colored leaves as they fell in fluttering clusters from the trees. ❦ Fall was also apple time, for cider and cobblers and smooth apple butter. Sometimes we would peel a stray apple and carve a face into it and hang it up to dry. Three weeks later the apple would have been transformed into an hilarious face. A body dressed in miniature clothes completed the doll. ❦ I used to watch my mother and grandmother sit at the kitchen table peeling apples by the dozen. What we didn't eat went into the freezer for stewed apples and pies later on. They would take a sharp knife in one hand, an apple in the other, and in what seemed to me like lightning speed, they would peel around and around

Fall Harvest

the apple until a long, single, curly strand of peel fell off and a naked apple magically appeared. ❦ I was convinced that one of the rites of passage to womanhood in my household was to be able to peel an apple from stem to core without breaking the curl, and I practiced and practiced until I, too, could take my place in that harvest ritual. It was around the kitchen table that I first learned about family legends and about the facts of life, and it was here that I first experienced the joy of shared work and shared laughter. ❦ And so, when my daughter asks why we're sitting there peeling apples to put in the freezer when we can just as easily buy them later on, I smile and answer with a story about her great-grandmother. She grimaces, but she listens as she peels around and around an apple.

Apple-Head Dolls

Finally, after many years, I have apples on my apple trees. Since the first blossoms appeared in spring, it has been a race to see if the apples would ripen before the squirrels ate them all. My crop dwindled from over a hundred to about fifteen, but the apples were delicious and were from my very own apple tree, so I was proud and happy.

I saved a few of the apples to make dolls. I had intended to give them as Christmas gifts and even made a Santa Claus from one of the heads, but I like them so much it's going to be hard to give them away. They have *personality*. Maybe by the time Christmas is here I won't be so attached and can give them up. But then again, maybe not.

TIME: 3–4 weeks for the apple to dry, 20 minutes to carve the apple, and 4 hours to make and dress the doll

COST: ☆

MATERIALS:

 Hard apples (Granny Smiths are good)

 14-gauge wire

 Pipe cleaners

 Adhesive tape

 Quilt batting

 Scraps of denim and calico

 Scraps of black vinyl (for boots)

 Gold wire (for glasses)

 Yarn or cotton (for hair)

 Small pieces of felt

DIFFICULTY: ✄ ✄ ✄ ✄

SHELF LIFE: Indefinite, if apple is dried properly

MAKING THE HEAD

1. Carefully peel an apple, removing as much skin as possible and leaving a smooth, rounded finish.
2. Mentally divide the apple into thirds horizontally. The eyes will go on the top-third line, the mouth on the bottom-third line, and the nose in the middle.
3. Carve a triangular nose, slits for eyes, eyebrows, a mouth, a chin, and dimples.
4. Bend a 12-inch (30-cm) piece of 14-gauge wire in half. Insert the wire all the way through the apple, leaving a small loop at the top.
5. Hang the apple in a dry, well-ventilated place. Allow to dry for 2 weeks.
6. After 2 weeks the apple will be soft and doughy. Press on either side of the nose to make it more prominent.
7. Allow to dry for another 1–2 weeks.

MAKING THE BODY

1. After the head is thoroughly dry, it is time to make the body. Begin with the arms. Take a 6-inch (15-cm) piece of wire or pipe cleaner. Center it horizontally just below the apple

head and secure it to the vertical wire with adhesive tape. Put a small amount of quilt batting around each arm to fill them out. Wrap with adhesive tape.

2. Make the torso by putting batting around the center of the wire. The torso should be 3 inches (8 cm) long, measuring from the bottom of the apple. Wrap with tape.

3. Below the bottom of the torso, separate the wires to form legs. Each leg should be approximately 3 inches (8 cm) long. Stuff and wrap as you did the torso and arms (photo A).

C

A

DRESSING THE DOLLS

How you dress the dolls depends entirely on what kind of character you want. These dolls are fairly sturdy and can be dressed and redressed in different outfits. You can probably find store-bought doll clothes to fit your homemade doll, and you can certainly find accessories such as glasses, hats, and the like.

You can make a house full of apple-head dolls in such clothing as overalls, shirts, skirts, dresses, pants, and boots. This is an ideal Christmas craft if you make a Santa outfit (photos B and C).

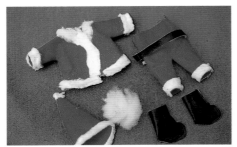

B

General directions: Make ⅛-inch (.3-cm) seams, and run a zigzag stitch over any raw edges.

Hair: This can be made from cotton balls or from yarn. Because apple-head dolls look like very old, wrinkled people, white or light gray hair looks best.

Glasses: Bend gold wire into eyeglass shapes.

Boots: Stitch boots right sides out. Stuff with cotton or batting, and push legs down into boot.

Scented
Pot Holders
🌰

Returning from vacation always brings mixed blessings. I'm happy to be back, but the garden has suffered greatly while I was gone. Why is it that weeds always grow so much faster than flowers? I weed until the mosquitoes begin nibbling on my legs, then trim and prune until they begin chewing in earnest.

In cleaning the herb bed I cut back enormous branches of lemon balm that seem to have grown ten feet while I was away. I'm too frugal to waste anything, particularly out of the garden, so I bring these branches inside to stuff pot holders and hot pads. When you put warm containers on top of them, the heat brings out the fragrance of the herbs.

along 3 sides and turn right side out. (If you're making hot pads rather than pot holders, omit the ring.)

3. Cut batting into an 11-inch (28-cm) square.
4. Insert batting into sewn square, smoothing it down as evenly as possible.
5. Insert 3–4 tablespoons of highly scented dried herbs.
6. Turn down edges of remaining side and slipstitch closed, securing raw edges inside, and catching piping in place.
7. Sew a 4-inch (10 cm) square around the center of the pad through all thicknesses, essentially "quilting" it so the batting won't slip and the herbs remain evenly distributed.

A

Variations: The variations on this craft are endless. If you can sew well enough to make a bag, you can make any number of scented gifts. Consider the following: Quilted bread-basket liner filled with rosemary · Christmas place mats filled with pine needles · Quilted jewelry case filled with potpourri · Child's bean bag in the shape of a gingerbread man filled with ground cinnamon sticks · Pincushion stuffed with rosemary (the leaves are supposed to help keep needles and pins sharp)

TIME: 45 minutes
COST: ☆
MATERIALS:
    Fabric ("panel" fabric is wonderful for this)
    Piping (optional)
    Small wooden ring (optional)
    Needle and thread or sewing machine
    Quilt batting
    Dried herbs
DIFFICULTY: ✂ ✂ ✂
SHELF LIFE: Indefinite

1. Cut fabric (photo A) into 12-inch (30-cm) squares.
2. Place 2 squares of fabric right sides together. If edging is desired, sandwich piping between fabric, with raw edge toward fabric edges. If you wish to be able to hang them, insert wooden ring through piping before stitching, and catch it in a small loop at an upper corner of the fabric. Sew

Peach Products
&

Lots of people talk about things being peach-colored, but the orangish hue that passes for "peach" looks as little like a real peach as a canned peach tastes like the real thing. A good peach, covered with tiny fuzz, is the color of sunshine and rain and good, rich earth. You simply can't copy it. Just as the color is almost impossible to duplicate, so is that intensely sweet fragrance of a ripe peach picked fresh off the tree.

Coming home from the mountains, we followed an old blue pickup truck through miles of winding roads. It was piled high with layers and layers of peaches. When it finally turned into the driveway of a small farmhouse, we turned in too, and talked the driver into selling us a basketful of peaches.

It was a case of my stomach—and good intentions—running away with me. A bushel of peaches is a lot of peaches, and once this fruit is ripe, you have to work with it quickly because it can go bad almost overnight.

I pickled and jammed and breaded my way through that big basket, putting enough in the freezer and the pantry shelves to give away for months. But the biggest and most delicious peach of all I saved to slice over ice cream and savor bite by bite. Now that's food for the gods!

Pickled Peaches

TIME: 1–1½ hours

COST: ☆ to ☆☆

MATERIALS:

   ½ peck (4 liter) peaches (14–15 medium to large size)

   Cheesecloth

   3 cinnamon sticks

   2 tablespoons whole allspice

   5 whole cloves

   Cotton string

   1 cup (250 ml) water

   4 cups (1 liter) sugar

   1½ cups (375 ml) rice vinegar

   2 1-quart (1-liter) or 4 1-pint (500-ml) jars with lids and bands

DIFFICULTY: ✂ ✂ ✂ ✂

SHELF LIFE: Indefinite

1. Place peaches in boiling water for 45 seconds. Remove from water and peel; skin should slip off easily.
2. Cut a piece of cheesecloth 6 inches (15 cm) square. Place spices in center of cloth and tie with cotton string.
3. Put spice bag, water, sugar, and vinegar in saucepan and bring to a boil. Add peaches and simmer for 25 minutes, or until tender.
4. Clean jars thoroughly and place in hot water until ready to use. When peaches and syrup are ready, dry jars and fill with peaches and syrup within ⅛ inch (.3 cm) of top, making sure to pack as many peaches into the jar as possible. They tend to shrink during processing and will float toward the top of the jar.
5. Place jars in a water bath and process for 10 minutes. (For further instructions on processing, see Basic Techniques, page 126.)

Peach Bread

I don't usually like baking cakes and breads with peaches—they seem to get all mushy and lose that delicate peach flavor. This recipe, though, uses the peaches as a middle layer, almost like a filling. It is also easy to make, incredibly delicious to eat, and nice to freeze to give away later.

TIME: 1½ hours

COST: ☆

MATERIALS:

    2 cups (500 ml) sliced fresh peaches

    3 teaspoons cinnamon

    2¼ cups (560 ml) sugar

    4 eggs

    1 cup (250 ml) vegetable oil

    3 cups (750 ml) flour

    1 teaspoon salt

    1 tablespoon baking powder

    ⅓ cup (80 ml) pineapple juice

    1 teaspoon vanilla extract

    1 teaspoon almond extract

    5 small loaf pans

DIFFICULTY: ✂ ✂

SHELF LIFE: Several weeks in the freezer

1. Preheat oven to 350° F (177° C).
2. Slice peaches and mix with cinnamon and ¼ cup (60 ml) of the sugar.
3. Beat eggs, remaining sugar, and oil together until well blended.
4. Mix dry ingredients together.
5. Alternately add dry ingredients and pineapple juice to egg mixture, mixing well after each addition.
6. Mix in extracts.
7. Grease 5 small loaf pans. Using half the batter, put an equal amount in each pan.
8. Divide the peach mixture evenly among the pans, pouring it on top of the batter.
9. Pour the remaining batter over the peaches, being careful to distribute it evenly.
10. Bake for 45–50 minutes, or until loaves test done. Let cool for 10 minutes before removing from pans.

Peach Jam

Two fruits can create a blend of flavors that is often better than either one used alone. Try mixing blackberries or blueberries with the peaches for a heavenly combination of colors and tastes.

TIME: 1 hour
COST: ☆ to ☆☆
MATERIALS:
  4 cups (1 liter) fresh peaches, sliced paper thin
  1 large tart green apple, sliced
  2 tablespoons lemon juice
  2 tablespoons cornstarch
  4 cups (1 liter) sugar
  Canning jars
DIFFICULTY: ✂ ✂
SHELF LIFE: Indefinite

1. Put sliced fruits in a saucepan with the lemon juice, cornstarch, and sugar.
2. Bring to a boil, then reduce heat and cook on medium until mixture has thickened, stirring often. *Note:* The length of time it takes to thicken depends on how ripe the fruit is and the exact amounts of fruit used. If desired, you can speed the thickening process by adding another tablespoon of cornstarch.
3. Place in hot, clean jelly jars and process for 10 minutes. (For further instructions on processing, see Basic Techniques, page 126.)

Vegetable Strings
❧

My mother left The Basket on my doorstep one morning full of beans from her garden. They were beautiful and so fresh they looked almost perky, but she brought me a lot of beans, much more than the family can eat in one or two weeks.

I remembered that some old-timey gardeners used to make "leather britches," strings of green beans that they would let dry then cook as they needed. They were decorative as well as useful. Last year on a trip to New York City, I saw a new twist on leather britches. A designer had strung green beans, small pieces of corn, bay leaves, and red chili peppers. Great idea!—and perfect for the windows in my sister's house in the country.

Make sure you don't use string that will rot easily or your entire craft will fall apart in a matter of weeks. Instead, use quilting thread, fishing line, or dental floss. When the beans are first strung they will be fat and plump, but as they dry they tend to shrivel, so your vegetable string will shorten slightly. You can use beans that have started to shrivel, but do not use beans that are moldy or rotten.

TIME: 30 minutes for an 18-inch (45-cm) string
COST: ☆
MATERIALS:
  Craft needle
  Quilting thread, fishing line, or dental floss
  Green beans (50 per 18-inch [45-cm] string)
  40 small red chili peppers
  4 2-inch (5-cm) pieces of yellow corn on the cob
  40 bay leaves
DIFFICULTY: ✂
SHELF LIFE: 12 months (vegetables begin to look old after this)

1. Thread the craft needle with a double string of quilting thread, fishing line, or dental floss. Tie a knot at the end.
2. Pierce a green bean in the center and pull it to the end of the string until it rests on the knot. Wrap the string around

A

FALL HARVEST ✦ 83

the bean once to secure it; since this is the bottom of the string of vegetables, you don't want it to fall out.

3. String 10 beans.
4. String 10 red chili peppers on top of the beans.
5. Put a small piece of corn on top of the peppers.
6. String 10 whole bay leaves on top of the corn.
7. Repeat these layers 3 more times, finally adding an extra 10 beans on top (photo A, see page 82).
8. Tie a knot at the top of the vegetables. Make a loop for hanging at the end of the string.

Windowsill Herbs

There's nothing like a fall sky, so blue it makes you want to throw your head back and drink it in and save it for those long, gray days of winter that are coming.

Though it's beautiful outside today, I know that a killing frost is right around the corner and I have a lot of work to do in the garden. Since I hate to lose anything to a frost, I will spend the next few days potting and cutting and salvaging every herb I can from the garden.

There's no reason not to have fresh herbs throughout the winter months, and with a little advance planning I can pot up divisions of many of my tender herbs to keep on a sunny windowsill. With a little luck and care they will last through the winter until I can replant them in the garden next spring. If you don't have herbs from your own garden, you can usually find bargains at local nurseries, which are generally anxious to get rid of tender annuals at the end of the season. Some of the best choices for growing indoors include bay, chives, mint, parsley, rosemary, and thyme.

Herbs grown indoors need as much light as you can possibly give them. Choose the sunniest spot in the house to set up your winter herb garden. If you keep the herbs in a basket, you can even move it from window to window to take advantage of the greatest amount of light. Snuggled down into a long, flat basket, these small potted plants make an instant herb garden—a perfect gift for any cook.

TIME: 30 minutes
COST: ☆ to ☆☆☆ (depending on choice of basket)
MATERIALS:
    Small clay pots
    Pebbles or small gravel
    Potting soil
    Divisions of herbs
    Long, flat basket lined with plastic
DIFFICULTY: ✄
SHELF LIFE: Indefinite, with proper care

1. Prepare the clay pots by placing a thin layer of pebbles on

A

B

finally decided on a small gourd doll. It's so ugly it's cute and it makes me smile every time I look at it. I thought it might cheer her up as well.

Gourds have been used for centuries for everything from dippers to bowls. The amazing structure of a sturdy gourd allows it to get wet over and over and still last for years.

The number of crafts you can make from gourds is limited only by your imagination and your ability to grow or find the right-size gourds. Large gourds are fairly easy to find at roadside stands or farmer's markets; small ones are a great deal harder to find and are more expensive because they are so desirable for crafts.

It is easy to grow gourds if you have plenty of space and sunshine in your garden. I planted the seeds from a miniature gourd in a barrel on my deck and grew an eight-foot (2-m) vine.

Gourd Birdhouse

Gourds provide perfect nesting cavities for many kinds of birds. How you make your birdhouse—the size of hole you cut—and where you hang it up will in part determine the kind of bird it will attract. The following birds have been reported nesting in gourds: purple martins, house wrens, sparrows, chickadees, and bluebirds. Not only do these birdhouses attract desirable wildlife, they also make great natural decorations for the garden.

the bottom of each and 3–4 inches (8–10 cm) of potting soil over them.

2. Divide out a portion of a large, healthy herb from the garden. Dig it up carefully, separating the roots from the mother plant (photo A).
3. Place each division in a prepared pot, filling in around the sides with potting soil (photo B). Water thoroughly.
4. Repeat with as many herbs as you wish.
5. Place the pots in a plastic-lined basket.
6. Bring indoors and keep in a sunny window. Water to keep the soil evenly moist but not too wet.

Gourd Projects

When a friend was confined to bed for a few months, I wanted to give her a get-well present but couldn't decide what to take. Flowers die too quickly; balloons eventually lose all their air. I

TIME: 1 hour
COST: Free if you grow your own gourd
MATERIALS:
Large oval gourd
Pocketknife or electric drill
Keyhole saw
DIFFICULTY: ✂ ✂
SHELF LIFE: Indefinite

1. To clean the gourd, soak in water for 1 hour, then scrub the outside. (It is not necessary to clean the gourds to make birdhouses; it will depend on personal preference.)
2. With a pencil, draw a circle on the gourd for a hole. Make sure you position it correctly. If you put it too high on the slant, rain will enter. If you put it too low, baby birds can fall out of the nest. Make an initial hole with a pocketknife or electric drill, then use a keyhole saw to make the cut.
3. Using the knife or drill, make several holes on the bottom of the gourd for drainage, and at the top for hanging.
4. You can finish the outside of the gourd any way you wish, or you can leave it plain. How you finish it depends on who you're making the birdhouse for. If it's for the birds, they probably prefer it to be left plain. If you are doing it for yourself or a friend, you might prefer to paint or varnish it.

Gourd Spoons

TIME: 10 minutes
COST: Free if you grow your own gourd
MATERIALS:
Small gourd with 2–5 inch (5–13 cm) bulb and 3–4 inch
(8–10 cm) neck
Keyhole saw
Sandpaper
DIFFICULTY: ✂ ✂
SHELF LIFE: Indefinite

1. Using the keyhole saw, cut the gourd lengthwise.

2. Clean out the inside of the gourd.
3. Use the sandpaper to smooth the edges of the spoon.

Gourd Doll

TIME: 20 minutes
COST: ☆
MATERIALS:
¼ yard (23 cm) calico
Needle and thread or sewing machine
Handful of polyester stuffing
Small round gourd with short neck
Glue gun
Permanent marker
Several strands of yarn
DIFFICULTY: ✂ ✂ ✂
SHELF LIFE: Indefinite

1. Cut two pieces of calico 5 × 6 inches (13 × 15 cm) for the body. Cut two more pieces 1¼ × 4 inches (3 × 10 cm) for the arms. Sew the two body pieces, right sides together, along sides and one end. Turn right side out.
2. Fold one arm piece lengthwise, right sides together. Sew along the long side and across the bottom. Turn right side out and fill lightly with stuffing. Tack the open edge closed. Repeat for the other arm.
3. Lightly fill the inside of the body with the stuffing material. Do not pack it in too tightly—you want a floppy doll.
4. Take long basting stitches around the top of the bag and pull threads to gather top. "Try on" the head by placing the gourd on top of the body and adjust the gathers. When you're satisfied with the positioning, glue gourd head to the body.
5. Glue the arms to the sides of the body, close to the "neck."
6. Make eyes with permanent marker.
7. Glue wisps of short yarn pieces to the top of the head for hair.
8. Cut an 8-inch (20-cm) square from the calico. Fold in half, making a triangle, and wrap around the head like a kerchief. Overlap ends and glue at the chin.

Ten Tiny Trinkets

I love making and giving little things. My entire family shares my love of the diminutive, and our favorite part of Christmas is discovering tiny trinkets in our stockings. We draw names for stockings so that everyone stuffs one and receives one. Early Christmas morning we burst into the den, pull the stockings down from the front of the fireplace, and spend the next hour slowly unwrapping small gifts from our stockings.

My daughter loves her Christmas stocking so much that when her birthday rolled around, I created a birthday stocking out of pieces of silks and velvets and brocades, put a huge white satin bow at the top, and filled it with miniature gifts. It was a huge success, so much so that when my son's June birthday approached, he made it clear that he expected a birthday stocking too. So I went back to the sewing room, this time to make a birthday stocking boot from camouflage fabric and fake leather.

Little presents are fun to give because you can give so many of them. There are hidden dangers in stuffing stockings or giving away collections of small gifts, however, for small doesn't always mean inexpensive. Before you know it, you may have spent up to fifty dollars (£30) on a sock full of stuff.

With a little thought and creativity, though, you can stuff a stocking or give away a mini-mountain of gifts for very little money. The gifts included here cost almost nothing and can be made in a short amount of time. These are not fine pieces of art. They are "love" gifts, things you can give away whenever the mood strikes you to give someone a present or when you don't want to go to a friend's house empty-handed. Make them in your spare moments and keep a supply on hand for emergency "pick-me-ups." While you're waiting for a pot of water to boil for spaghetti, you can tie together a few stalks of wheat, glue a dried rosebud on one side and a small kitchen magnet on the other side, and you have a tiny trinket.

Many of these are easy versions of other crafts found in this book. Because they are quicker to make, they may also be better suited for children to do. Most can be used in a variety of ways—glued to a small magnet to put on the refrigerator, hung from a hook to brighten the kitchen window, placed on the Christmas tree, or used as decoration on a gift box. Give them away in a birthday stocking or make them to brighten your own kitchen window.

Ten Tiny Trinkets

Fireplace Herb Bundle · Corn-Shuck Babies · Tiny Pepper Wreath · Small String of Peppers and Bay Leaves · Mini Vine Wreath · Sheaf of Wheat with Rosebud · Tiny Tussie-mussie · Baby Gourd Arrangement · Pressed-Flower Note Cards · Rosemary Barbecue Wand

TIME: 1–10 minutes each

COST: ☆

MATERIALS:

    General materials for several crafts

    Assorted herbs

    Raffia or string

    Corn shucks

    Lightweight wire

    Dried chili peppers

    Bay leaves

    Small magnets

    Several strands of vine

    Small pieces of lace and ribbon

    Bits of dried and pressed flowers

    Wheat or dried grass

    Small gourd

    Paper

    Clear self-adhesive film

DIFFICULTY: ✂

SHELF LIFE: Varies from 3 weeks (rosemary barbecue wand) to indefinite (gourd arrangement)

FALL HARVEST & 89

FIREPLACE HERB BUNDLE

Take a small bunch (5–15 stalks) of herbs and cut the ends so that the pieces are no more than 6 inches (15 cm) long. Tie in the center with a piece of raffia or string. This is the perfect thing to do while trimming the herb garden. It is also a good way to use up annual herbs before the first frost of the season.

CORN-SHUCK BABIES

1. Put 3–4 pieces of corn shuck in water for 1 minute to soften.
2. Dry off the shucks. Take one piece and fold in half lengthwise and then fold in half crosswise. Repeat until you have a somewhat rounded "head."
3. Put the center of another shuck at the top of the "head" you

formed. Using a long, narrow (⅛-inch [.3-cm] wide) piece of shuck, tie the second shuck underneath the chin to look like a blanket draped around a baby's head. This is a fairly crude doll, but it can be dressed up as you wish. You can make a slit in the center of another shuck, pull it over the doll's head, and tie around the waist. You can make arms by using a thicker piece of shuck to tie under the chin, allowing the ends to stick out to either side.

SMALL STRING OF PEPPERS AND BAY LEAVES

Make a loop at the bottom of a 6-inch (15-cm) piece of wire. String 10 small dried chili peppers, 10 bay leaves, and 10 more peppers. Make a loop at the top, cutting off any excess wire. This can be glued to a small magnet for the refrigerator, hung on a small nail at a window, or used as a southwestern-style Christmas tree ornament.

MINI VINE WREATH

Wrap a long strand of vine (honeysuckle, jasmine, kudzu, wisteria, or wild grape) around your hand to get a basic circle shape. Take another strand and weave over and under, securing the ends under pieces of the wreath. Decorate with a small ribbon or glue on small dried flowers.

SHEAF OF WHEAT WITH ROSEBUD

Make a small bundle of 5–6 stalks of wheat or dried grass. Put a single dried rosebud in the center and tie together with a piece of raffia. This makes a lovely decoration for a gift box.

TINY TUSSIE-MUSSIE

Make a miniature bouquet with 3–4 tiny dried flowers. Gather a small piece of lace trim around the bouquet and tie with a color-coordinated ribbon. Glue to a magnet and use on the refrigerator.

edges. This makes a beautiful gift card when tied on with thin satin ribbon.

ROSEMARY BARBECUE WAND
Snip 5–6 pieces of fresh rosemary. Tie at the top with a piece of cotton string. This adds a delicious hint of rosemary when used to spread sauce on meat or vegetables before grilling.

BABY GOURD ARRANGEMENT
Glue a tiny bundle of dried flowers to the front of a small gourd. Or, to make it look just like the "grown-up" gourd flower containers, cut a small hole in the front of the gourd using a sharp pocketknife and glue the bundle in the hole.

TINY PEPPER WREATH
Take a 10-inch (25-cm) piece of wire that is stiff but bends easily. Make a loop at one end. Push the wire through the center of small dried chili peppers, making a string. Carefully bend this into a round or heart-shaped wreath. Going through the bottom wire loop, make another loop at the top and form a hook for hanging.

PRESSED-FLOWER NOTE CARDS
Cut a piece of good-quality $8\frac{1}{2} \times 11$-inch (21×28-cm) paper into quarters and fold each quarter in half, then in half again, making a card one-eighth the size of the original paper. Place a small pressed flower on the front of the card and cover the entire front with a piece of clear self-adhesive film. Trim the

Deep-Dish Apple Pie

ॐ

Finally, the weather has begun to turn cool. I walked through the woods at my parents' house, lost in the memories of playing there when I was a young girl. The woods look different, the trees don't seem to be quite as tall, and the ravines that seemed too wide to jump when I was a child are easy to step over now.

Many things in the woods have not changed at all, however. My imagination still runs free and wild through the woods and on a whim I can be an Indian princess or a sturdy pioneer woman. But as I walk on and on, reality tugs gently on the apron strings of my imagination, and reluctantly I turn my steps toward my house to welcome my own children home from school. Suddenly inspired by the crisp fall afternoon and the memories of my childhood, I decide to fix Grandma's deep-dish apple pie for dinner and, considerably cheered at the thought of this treat in store, I return home happy and flushed with a touch of autumn.

TIME: 45 minutes

COST: ☆

MATERIALS:

   3–4 large, tart apples (Granny Smiths are best)

   ¼ cup (60 ml) brown sugar

   1 cup (250 ml) sugar

   1 cup (250 ml) flour

   1 stick (125 ml) butter or margarine

   1 teaspoon cinnamon

DIFFICULTY: ✂ ✂

SHELF LIFE: 2–3 days in the refrigerator; best if eaten hot from the oven

1. Preheat oven to 350°F (177°C).

2. Peel and slice apples, and place in a 9-inch (23-cm) glass pie pan. Sprinkle with brown sugar.
3. Mix sugar, flour, and butter together until mixture looks like coarse crumbs.
4. Sprinkle flour mixture over apples. Sprinkle cinnamon over top.
5. Bake 35–45 minutes, or until apples are tender and top has browned nicely. Excellent served with a scoop of vanilla ice cream.

Seeds from the Garden

ॐ

I welcome the autumn season and the chance to put my garden to rest for the coming months. Although I passionately love to garden, it's nice to be able to step back and look at it from a new perspective. I dig up and discard what I didn't particularly like one year and sit and dream about what I want the garden to look like the next year.

Now is the time to plan for next year. At the same time that a plant is dying, it is also preparing new life in the form of seeds. Seeds are nature's gift to us. Without harming the plant or detracting from its strength or beauty, we can capture seeds and plant again to perpetuate the glory of the garden. A seed, lovingly cared for by the gardener, will produce a bounteous harvest.

Giving away seeds from your garden is fun, easy, and economical, but be smart when you do so. Not all seeds are suitable for saving. Seeds from hybrid plants will not stay true to the parent plant and often revert back to something fairly undesirable. Different plants go to seed at different times of the year, so you can collect seeds from June through October or November. You need to collect them when they are fully ripe but before they scatter. To determine optimum collecting times, check the plants every few days toward the end of their growth cycle. Some flowers go from bloom to seed in only a few weeks, while others take several months. Mature seed pods look different for different species, but in general they will turn from a light to a dark color and will expand in size.

Once you've gathered the seeds you can, of course, simply put them in an old envelope, scribble the name on it, and give it away. But presentation is important. Why not personalize seed packages using colored pens or even watercolors? Find pictures of old-fashioned seed packages to get some ideas, or include a few philosophies about the wonder of seeds. But be practical, too, and make sure you include—perhaps on the back—instructions for sowing and growing that particular plant.

The following plants produce abundant seeds that are easy to gather and store and generally have good germination:

Black-eyed Susan · Butterfly weed · Cleome · Coleus · Cosmos · Globe amaranth · Marigold · Moonflower · Purple coneflower · Salvia · Snapdragon · Vinca · Zinnias

TIME: 1½ hours to clean seeds, create envelopes, and package seeds
LEAD TIME: 2 weeks for seeds to dry thoroughly
COST: ☆
MATERIALS:
    Seeds from the garden or roadside
    Small envelopes (invitation size)
DIFFICULTY: ✂
SHELF LIFE: Varies from species to species. To be on the safe side, store seeds for only 1 year.

1. Collect mature seed heads from the garden or roadside and spread on clean newspaper in a dry, well-ventilated area.
2. Allow to dry for a few days to 2 weeks.
3. If insects are a problem, place the seed heads in a paper or plastic bag with a pesticide strip and store in a cool, dry place for several days.
4. If the seed heads have split or cracked open, place in a paper bag and shake vigorously to dislodge the seeds. Some species produce seed heads that will have to be cut open and the seeds removed by hand.
5. Remove as much chaff and litter as possible before storing or packaging the seeds. A bit of litter won't hurt, but the cleaner the seed collection, the easier the planting.
6. Decorate envelopes as desired. If painting or drawing is not your favorite—or most accomplished—skill, you can press the appropriate flower and secure it to the envelope with clear self-adhesive film (see step 4 of Pressed-Flower Place Cards, page 48). See the list below for suggested sayings to include on your packages.
7. Place a small amount of seeds in your prepared envelope or package. Include sowing and growing instructions.

SAYINGS FROM OLD-FASHIONED SEED PACKAGES

"A seed of summer, to keep through a winter, to plant in spring . . . eternal bud"

"Seeds—what could they be? A thought from my garden"

"A summer secret: A seed or two from me to you, to plant at leisure, yields a garden's pleasure"

"Herein some seeds—hope not weeds"

FALL HARVEST ❦ 95

"Seeds, those little souls of plants in which the whole and compleat tree . . . though invisible to our dull sense, is yet perfectly and entirely wrapped up"

It is considered good luck to spread vinca in front of a bridal couple, so throw vinca leaves and petals instead of rice.

Planted outside the garden gate, vinca is an invitation to visit the garden.

Aster leaves burned in the fireplace were thought to keep away evil spirits.

Peony seeds were thought to keep newborn babies safe from harm.

Peonies preserve harvest from danger.

Peonies ward off storms, demons, and nightmares.

The peony is the Japanese symbol of happy marriage.

To dream of daisies in spring brings months of good luck.

Cosmos, a symbol of harmony, means "ordered universe."

He who is anointed with the oil of snapdragon will become famous.

The heart-shaped leaves of pansies are said to cure a broken heart. The word *pansy* is thought to come from the French *pensée,* referring to thoughts.

Sending a bouquet of phlox to a friend means sweet dreams and a declaration of love.

Dried-Flower Strings

&

One of my favorite ways to spend an autumn afternoon is to work on dried flower crafts. Several years ago, after spending the day making gifts from dried flowers, the kitchen table was a mess. There were bits and pieces of dried flowers everywhere and I sighed as I got out the trash can. The blossoms were so fine that I hated to throw them away. They just had such short stems it was difficult to use them for anything.

Right before I discarded the flowers I had a sudden inspiration. Why not tape the short ends together and string them together to create long floral hangings?

I quickly grabbed a handful of short-stemmed dried statice and baby's breath and held them end to end so that the

flowers were on the outside. I wrapped the center stems with floral tape and stood back to look. They looked pretty strange. Quickly I made several more and then took thread and strung them together. The result was quite pleasing, and I kept adding more and more until I had a full floral ball, perfect for hanging from a Victorian light fixture or a chandelier.

But do note that these are extremely fragile, since most dried flowers are fairly brittle. I suggest that you do not put these strings in a vulnerable place. Although a door knob may seem like a perfect spot to hang one of these, it is not a good idea unless that door is seldom used.

TIME: 30 minutes
COST: ☆
MATERIALS:
    Pieces of dried flowers
    Floral tape
    Needle and strong thread
DIFFICULTY: ✄ ✄
SHELF LIFE: Indefinite

A

B

1. Take 2 small bunches of dried flowers (photo A); clip stems, if necessary, to no more than 3 inches (8 cm) long. Put the stems side by side, with one bundle of flowers pointing left, the other pointing right.
2. Wrap the stems with green floral tape. This will create small "barbells" of flowers (photo B). Make 15 or 16 of these barbells for a 6-inch (16-cm) ball.
3. Using strong thread (quilting thread, dental floss, or clear fishing line), string through the center of these bundles. Alternate colors and shades in order to create a pleasing arrangement.
4. Tie securely at the top and make a loop in the string for hanging.

Wheat and Roses

One of my favorite housewarming gifts is a simple sheaf of twisted wheat tied with a braid of raffia. Wheat has long been the symbol of abundance and having a sheaf of wheat in your home meant that you would never go hungry.

Wheat has become a favorite plant for many floral designers and can be used in a variety of ways. "Planted" with dried roses it makes a simple but elegant arrangement. In stores and through mail-order catalogs, these wheat arrangements are very expensive. Yet they are not difficult to make, and even if you don't grow wheat, you can buy dried bundles of wheat fairly inexpensively. If you don't have easy access to wheat, many dried field grasses can be substituted.

TIME: 30 minutes
COST: ☆ to ☆☆☆
MATERIALS:
    10-inch (25-cm) clay pot
    Styrofoam

About 50 stalks of wheat
24 dried roses
Spanish or green sheet moss
Raffia

DIFFICULTY: ✂ ✂ ✂

SHELF LIFE: Indefinite

1. Cut a block of Styrofoam to fit into the bottom of the clay pot snugly. The top of the Styrofoam should be even with the top of the pot.
2. Stick the wheat stalks into the center of the Styrofoam so that the stems stand about 16–18 inches (40–45 cm) above the pot rim. Arrange the wheat evenly but in an open, airy fashion.
3. After the wheat has been arranged in the center, make a complete, evenly spaced circle of roses around the wheat.

This can be tricky, particularly if the roses do not have straight stems, as often happens. Keep working at it until the tops are even, and don't worry about the bottoms. You do not need to fill the entire pot for this craft. Keep everything toward the center.

4. Cover the top of the Styrofoam with the moss, being careful not to knock over any of the wheat or roses.

Variations: Place 25–30 straight stalks of wheat close together in Styrofoam in a clay pot. Make sure that the flowering heads are even. Tie toward the top with a single piece of raffia. Or line up short pieces of wheat (10–14 inches [25–35 cm] tall) until the heads are even. Cut off the bottom of the stems so that they too are even. Make a bundle, then twist it a couple of inches (5 cm) below the heads to make a sheaf. At the point where you twisted the stems, tie with a thin piece of braided raffia.

Winter days are made for warm slippers and cups of hot cider. It is a time for staying indoors and creating a haven from the cold weather—a perfect time for doing crafts. From the middle of November until the time I need to clear the table to set it for Christmas dinner, every available flat surface in our house is covered with crafts. I suppose that to the untrained eye it might look like total chaos, a real mess. However, if you look closely, you can tell that the black stuff on the table is not just dirt but is actually potting soil for the miniature terrariums, and the long strands of thin, shiny material are not spiderwebs but bits of corn silk for the corn-shuck angels. ❧ Bright flowers from the garden, dried months earlier, bring a particular cheerfulness to the house. They seemed so ordi-

Winter Treasures

nary by the end of the summer, just another bright spot in the garden. Now, with the garden put to rest for the winter, these strawflowers and globe amaranth appear exciting and exotic. Combined with bits of lace and ribbon, these carefully preserved summer flowers will add a touch of elegant country to the Christmas tree. ❧ The winter holidays provide the perfect excuse for gift giving and make it easy to justify indulging in an orgy of crafting. The cold season is a time for spending long hours doing intricate crafts, your hands constantly busy, your thoughts perhaps a million miles away. It is a time for dreaming about next year's garden, for determining that this time the garden will be the most beautiful ever; and, after the holidays are over and the children have gone back to school, it is a time for bringing out the seed catalogs to begin to make those dreams come true.

Corn-Shuck Dolls

Dolls made from corn husks were sometimes the only toys that pioneer children had to play with. Though lacking the "realistic" features of today's plastic dolls or of expensive porcelain antiques, corn-shuck figures have a simplicity and charm difficult to duplicate with other materials. These small angels with their ruffled skirts and bendable arms look captivating on the mantel or hanging from the Christmas tree.

Field corn (grown for fodder) produces wide, heavy husks that are better suited to corn-shuck crafts than those from sweet corn. If you don't have the space, time, or inclination to grow field corn yourself, the shucks can sometimes be found in grocery stores, for these husks are also used in making

tamales and other Mexican dishes, or can be ordered through a supplier (see page 151).

The shucks will show a surprising amount of variation. Shucks that were close to the cob will be thin, while the outer layers will be much thicker. Some will be smooth, others will show thick ridges.

Once you have the materials set up, it's easier to make two or three dolls at one time than to make them individually.

TIME: 2 hours for 2 dolls
COST: ☆ (using homegrown shucks)
MATERIALS:
　　10–12 corn shucks from field corn
　　Paper towels
　　Craft scissors
　　⅞-inch (2-cm) Styrofoam ball
　　Toothpick or plastic straw
　　Strong thread or twine
　　Chenille strips or pipe cleaners
　　Glue gun and glue
　　Embroidery floss
DIFFICULTY: ✂ ✂ ✂ ✂
SHELF LIFE: Indefinite

PRELIMINARY PREPARATIONS
1. Select 10–12 clean shucks (photo A, page 103) and soak in warm water for approximately 10 minutes.
2. Remove shucks, shake off excess water, and place on paper towels to dry.
3. To make corn-shuck angels, cut wings (about 3 inches [8 cm] across and slightly longer top to bottom) out of a piece of thick shuck and place between the pages of a book to dry flat.

MAKING THE HEAD
1. Put the Styrofoam ball on the toothpick or a piece of plastic straw, making sure the Styrofoam is secure.
2. From a relatively thin, smooth shuck, cut a piece 5 inches (13 cm) long by 1½ inches (4 cm) wide. Tie a piece of

thread around the middle of the shuck, pulling it tight to form gathers and leaving both ends free.

3. Center gathered part of the shuck on top of the Styrofoam ball and gently spread it out to cover the ball, both in front and in back. Make sure that the sides overlap since the shuck will shrink some as it dries.

4. Tie the shuck securely at the base of the ball around the toothpick, forming the doll's neck (photo B).

MAKING THE ARMS

1. Cut two chenille strips each about 3 inches (8 cm) long.

2. Cut two pieces of corn shuck each 3 inches (8 cm) long by 2 inches (5 cm) wide.

3. Center the chenille strips on the shuck and roll up until the shuck completely covers the strips. Tie securely at each end, leaving a short piece to form the "hands."

4. Glue the center of the arms to the center of the back of the neck (photo C).

MAKING THE BODY

1. Cut the remaining 8–10 shucks into 1½-inch (4-cm) wide strips. Put the center of one strip just to the side of the head and fold downward at a slight angle, beginning to form the body and skirt of the doll (photo D).

2. Place the center of another strip on the opposite side of the head and fold down.

3. Continue to crisscross strips across the shoulders, alternating sides and adding enough layers to make a full body and skirt.

4. Secure the husks by tying tightly at the waist with a piece of strong thread or twine. You may find it helpful to secure the body temporarily with a piece of chenille so you'll have both hands free to tie the thread or twine tightly. Once the thread is in place, remove the chenille.

5. Make a belt by tying a piece of thin husk over the thread.

6. To make a curly skirt, carefully slit the husks of the skirt with scissors while the shucks are still wet. The thin pieces of shucks will naturally curl upward. Cut across the bottom of the skirt to even up all the edges.

A

B

C

D

FINISHING TOUCHES

1. To make an angel, glue wings to the back of the doll.
2. Make hair by wrapping brown or black embroidery floss around a 4-inch (10-cm) piece of cardboard. Carefully slip the thread off the board and tie securely at the center. Slit loops at ends to make straight hair.
3. "Comb out" hair to make the threads as smooth as possible.
4. Glue hair to the head, making sure to bring it slightly forward to give a nice, soft touch to the doll's face (photo E).
5. Give the doll added color and interest by having her hold various treasures such as tiny wrapped presents, a miniature bundle of dried flowers, a small herb wreath, or a tiny basket full of scented herbs or potpourri.

E

Variations: The basic corn-shuck doll can be decorated differently to be used for various holidays throughout the year. She can hold a heart for Valentine's Day, a basket of tiny eggs for Easter, even a miniature pumpkin for Thanksgiving!

If you don't like the ruffled skirt look, choose a wide shuck and carefully cover the entire skirt, making it smooth.

If you want to be entirely authentic and not use any synthetic products, form the head by folding pieces of cornshuck into a round ball, use folded shucks instead of the toothpick or straw, make the arms out of rolled shucks, and use corn silk for the hair. The face may not be quite as smooth and symmetrical as when you use a Styrofoam ball, but the doll will be all natural.

Cranberry-Basil Jelly & Whole Wheat Basil Bread

When the weather starts to turn cold, I can't bear the thought of all my annual herbs dying with the first frost, so I dig them up and bring them inside where they will also die but more slowly. I know that many herbs are not suitable for growing indoors, but I also know that even with moderate interior light conditions I can extend the life of such plants as basil by many months, making it possible to have fresh basil leaves at my disposal even as late as the end of November.

Basil makes lovely jelly and herb bread for Christmas presents. The jelly, when processed properly, will last for years. The bread, which I make in small loaves, can be stored in the freezer for a few weeks until I am ready to give it away. By the third week in December, my freezer is usually full of small loaves of different kinds of breads. It is such fun to pack fabric-lined baskets full of these loaves and small jars of bright jelly and present them to favorite friends.

Cranberry-Basil Jelly

TIME: 1 hour

COST: ☆

MATERIALS:

½ cup (125 ml) fresh basil leaves, lightly packed

2½ cups (625 ml) white sugar

2 cups (500 ml) cranberry juice

1¾ oz. (49 g) powdered fruit pectin (1 package)

8 4-ounce (125 ml) jelly jars and lids

Scraps of green calico

Red ribbon

DIFFICULTY: ✄ ✄ ✄

SHELF LIFE: Indefinite

1. Boil cranberry juice until it is reduced to 1½ cups (375 ml).
2. Make a basil infusion by putting the leaves in ¼ cup (60 ml) of boiling water and allowing to steep for 15–30 minutes. Strain.
3. Add the sugar to the cranberry juice and bring to a boil, stirring until the sugar is dissolved. Add the basil infusion.
4. Bring the liquid to a boil again and add the pectin. Bring to a rolling boil and boil for exactly 1 minute.
5. Pour into sterilized jelly jars and process for five minutes. Remove jars from water and allow to cool completely. (For further instructions on processing, see Basic Techniques, page 126.)
6. Cut rounds of green calico approximately 2 inches (5 cm) wider than jar tops and put over lids. Tie with red ribbon.

Whole Wheat Basil Bread

TIME: 4 hours

COST: ☆

MATERIALS:

   1 package (7 g) dry yeast
   ¼ cup (60 ml) warm water
   2 tablespoons sugar
   4 tablespoons unsalted butter
   1 cup (250 ml) warm buttermilk
   1 cup (250 ml) warm water
   ¼ cup (60 ml) honey
   2½ teaspoons salt
   2½ cups (625 ml) unbleached flour
   2½–3 cups (625–750 ml) whole wheat flour
   ½ cup (125 ml) minced fresh basil
   ½ cup (125 ml) sliced almonds
   1 tablespoon olive oil
   1 garlic clove, crushed
   Pinch cayenne pepper
   ¼ cup (60 ml) grated Parmesan cheese
   Foil or plastic wrap

DIFFICULTY: ✂ ✂ ✂

SHELF LIFE: 2–3 weeks in freezer

1. Dissolve yeast in ¼ cup (60 ml) warm water, add 2 tablespoons sugar, and allow mixture to sit 10 minutes, or until bubbly.
2. Mix the butter, buttermilk, water, honey, and salt and add to the yeast mixture with the unbleached flour. Mix well.
3. Gradually add the whole wheat flour 1 tablespoon at a time, combining until the mixture leaves the sides of the bowl and is only slightly sticky. Add the basil and almonds while mixing in flour.
4. Knead 5–7 minutes. Place in a greased bowl and turn once to grease all sides. Let rise in a warm place 1–1½ hours.
5. Punch down and divide into 2 round loaves or 6 small loaves. Allow to rise again 1 hour.
6. Make an oil wash by combining the olive oil, garlic, and pepper. Brush over the loaves and sprinkle with Parmesan cheese.
7. Bake at 350°F (177°C) for 50–60 minutes.
8. Allow to cool. Wrap with heavy plastic wrap or aluminum foil, or place small loaves in freezer bags. Freeze if necessary.

Miniature Ornaments

When I open up storage boxes of dried flowers, I am always amazed at the vibrant colors and strong shapes that some plants seem to hold almost indefinitely. The ten best dried garden flowers are baby's breath, cockscomb, globe amaranth, hydrangea, larkspur, lavender, rosebuds, statice, strawflower, and yarrow. For more information about dried flowers, refer to page 124.

Tiny tussie-mussies, finger-sized baskets, and miniature straw hats covered with bright dried flowers and colorful ribbons look charming on a tabletop Christmas tree and are perfect as quick gifts. When glued to small kitchen magnets they can be used year-round and are the perfect gift for those aunts and grandmothers who seem to have everything and are delighted to receive handmade gifts.

Straw-Hat Ornament

TIME: 6–8 minutes
COST: ☆
MATERIALS:
  Small straw hat (4–5 inches [10–13 cm] across)
  Small dried flowers
  ⅛-inch (.3-cm) wide ribbon to match flowers
  Glue gun and glue
  Ornament hooks or kitchen magnets
DIFFICULTY: ✂
SHELF LIFE: Indefinite

1. Glue small flowers around the hat, where the crown meets the brim.
2. Tie the ribbon into a bow and glue to hat, letting tails hang about 2 inches (5 cm) over brim.
3. Attach ornament hook to the front edge of the brim, or glue a magnet on the underside of the hat.

Tussie-mussie Ornament

TIME: 6–9 minutes
COST: ☆
MATERIALS:
  Small dried flowers
  Picks and wire (available at florists)
  Lace fabric or 2-inch (5-cm) wide lace trim
  ⅛-inch (.3-cm) wide ribbon to match flowers
  Ornament hook or kitchen magnet

DIFFICULTY: ✂
SHELF LIFE: Indefinite

1. Select 3 or 4 small dried flowers (photo A) and make a miniature bouquet. The bouquet should be tiny—perhaps only an inch (3 cm) across.
2. Take a florist's pick and wrap the wire around the stems of the flowers.
3. Cut a piece of lace 2 inches (5 cm) wide by 4 inches (10 cm) long and carefully gather it around the bouquet, allowing it to fluff out in a circle. Tie a bow with the ribbons underneath the flower heads, securing the gathers in the lace. Allow the tails of the ribbons to trail a couple of inches (5 cm).
4. Hook one end of an ornament hook under the ribbons or glue on a magnet.

A

Flower Basket Ornament

TIME: 4–6 minutes
COST: ☆
MATERIALS:
   Tiny basket
   Small dried flowers, including baby's breath
   Sprig of thyme
   Glue gun and glue
   1/8-inch (.3-cm) wide ribbon to match flowers
   Ornament hook or kitchen magnet
DIFFICULTY: ✂
SHELF LIFE: Indefinite

1. Spread some glue around the top edge of half the basket rim. Glue small, loose flowers around the rim. Repeat on the other half.
2. Put flowers with small stems still attached down into the basket. Be sure to add some baby's breath to give it a delicate, airy look. A little piece of thyme gives a nice touch of greenery and lends a spicy scent to the ornament. Secure the stemmed flowers with glue if necessary.
3. Tie a bow and glue to the front of the basket. Hang on the tree using an ornament hook or glue a magnet on one side.

Herb Wreath Bell Pull

Although miniature herb wreaths can be given as is, they can also be used in a variety of other ways. One of the most beautiful is to secure them to a bell pull of red satin ribbon. After Christmas the small wreaths can be used as flavoring in soups and stews.

If you live in a climate where everything dies back long before Christmastime, you will have to do a little advance planning. Make your wreaths before your herbs disappear for the winter—they ought to dry well and last a few months.

Some herbs will do better if they are dried in the microwave as soon as they are made into wreaths. Rosemary and thyme will air-dry just fine, but oregano tends to wilt and should be dried quickly. To dry these tiny wreaths, place in the microwave on high for 30 seconds to 2 minutes, depending on your microwave and the thickness of the wreath. Start with 30 seconds and increase the time gradually. Do not overcook or the wreaths will shatter.

You may sometimes find it necessary to use a wire circle to make the wreath form and then weave the herbs in and out of it. The project is easier this way, but there is a disadvantage—the wreath cannot be used for cooking unless the leaves are pulled off and used separately. *Caution: If you use a wire frame, do not dry in the microwave.*

TIME: 1½ hours

COST: ☆

MATERIALS:

> Thyme, rosemary, oregano, mint, or any other available herbs
>
> 2 yards (1.8 m) ⅛-inch (.3-cm) wide white or red satin ribbon
>
> 2¼ yards (2 m) 2-inch (5-cm) wide red satin ribbon

2¼ yards (2 m) very stiff fusible interfacing

Iron

Needle and thread or sewing machine

1¾ yards (1.5 m) 2-inch (5-cm) wide gathered calico trim

White glue

DIFFICULTY: ✂< ✂

SHELF LIFE: Wreaths will last 6–12 weeks; bell pull can be used year after year

MAKING THE WREATHS

1. Before your herbs go underground for winter, cut lengths of herbs as long as possible, preferably 10–12 inches (25–30 cm). Shorter pieces will also work, but you'll have to weave them in.
2. Weave together 2 pieces of the same herb to make a single long piece.
3. Gently bend this into a circle slightly less than 2 inches (5 cm) across and continue to weave in additional pieces until the wreath reaches desired thickness.
4. Secure the ends by tying a bow of narrow satin ribbon at the bottom of the wreath. If the wreath seems a little wobbly, it can be made more secure by weaving the ribbon through it.

MAKING THE BELL PULL

1. Cut 2 pieces of the wide red ribbon 25 inches (62 cm) long. Cut two pieces of heavy interfacing the same width and length. With a hot iron, secure interfacing to each piece of ribbon, making sure that the "glue" (usually shiny) side of the interfacing is next to the fabric. (If you've never used fusible interfacing, ask for directions at your craft or fabric store.)
2. To make the bow, fold one piece of the interfaced ribbon in half so you have a piece 12½ inches (31 cm) long. Stitch along each long edge. Fold again so that the raw edges and folded edge overlap 1 inch (3 cm) at the center back of the bow. Stitch edges together.
3. Fold a 5-inch (13-cm) piece of ribbon around the center of the bow. Secure by sewing into place.

4. Sew the gathered calico edging around the sides and bottom of the straight piece of interfaced ribbon, turning under the raw edge of ribbon at bottom. Place the bow at top center and sew into place.

ATTACHING THE WREATHS
1. Space 8 wreaths evenly along the length of the bell pull.
2. Secure them by gluing the backs of the small bows of each wreath to the bell pull. If you plan to use the wreaths for cooking, be careful not to get any glue on the herbs.
3. Glue an ornament hook to the back of the top center of the bell pull for hanging.

Variations: The wreaths can be used in many different ways. Tie them to a package, hang by slender ribbons in the kitchen window, or put them on the door of a dollhouse.

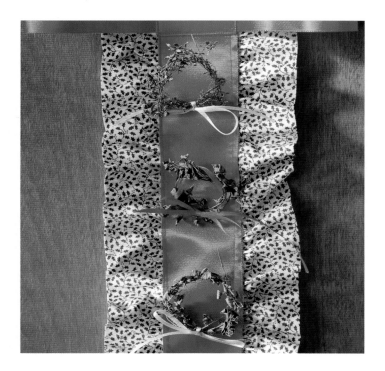

Evergreen Wreath
&

When I gather greens for decorations, the house finally begins to smell like Christmas. Simple evergreen wreaths adorned only with red nandina berries make an elegant decoration for the mantelpiece or the front door. There are several ways to make an evergreen wreath, but if you use a wire frame stuffed with damp sphagnum moss, the wreath will remain fresh-looking for over a month. It is a bit more difficult and time-consuming than simply wiring branches to a form, but the extra effort is well worth it to have a fresh wreath for such a long time.

You can weave ivy into long pieces to put around the fireplace and mantel. This requires very long pieces since after only a few days out of water the ivy starts to get dry and crisp. To make it last as long as possible (almost three weeks), I put large jars of water in baskets on either side of the fireplace and put the ends of the ivy in them.

It seems to be one of those inescapable rules that no matter how many greens you think you're going to need, you'll need twice as many. I once gathered what I thought was enough to make three wreaths and ended up going back out to gather again and again to make only one. The wreath seems to absorb everything you put on it. If you are running short, ask at a Christmas tree lot for any broken branches. There are usually plenty around, and they will make good fillers. Try to include some variegated evergreens as well, such as hollies, yellow or gold-leaf juniper, or spruce. When filled with evergreens, a 16-inch (40-cm) frame will measure about 36 inches (90 cm) across.

TIME: 1½–2 hours
COST: ☆
MATERIALS:
    Small bag of sphagnum moss

16-inch (40-cm) wire frame

Spool of plastic floral tape (1–2 inches [3–5 cm] wide—as
wide as possible)

Spruce, juniper, holly, pine, fir, boxwood—whatever evergreens are available

DIFFICULTY: ✂ ✂ ✂ ✂

SHELF LIFE: Approximately 3–4 weeks

C

1. Soak the sphagnum moss in a sink full of water. It absorbs
   water quickly but will look and smell a little rank in the
   process. After 10–15 minutes transfer the wet sphagnum
   moss from the sink to a large bowl or pan.
2. Place the wire frame (photo A) on newspapers and stuff as
   much wet moss as possible into the frame.
3. Wrap the plastic floral tape around the wire frame, effectively securing the moss (photo B). Continue until the moss
   and frame are completely covered.
4. Prepare the evergreen branches by stripping off the foliage
   at least 6 inches (15 cm) from the bottom of the stem.

A

B

Branches with a broad bottom end can be sharpened to a
point to make them easier to attach to the frame.

5. Begin filling the frame by slipping the ends of the branches
   in between the overlapping layers of floral tape (photo C).
   This is considerably easier than trying to pierce the tape
   with each branch.
6. Continue to add branches, going in the same direction
   so that the branches overlap one another and the flow of
   the wreath is continuous. Add evergreens until the wreath
   is very full and completely covered. Save branches with
   brightly colored berries to add to the bottom of the wreath.
   Add variegated evergreen branches as highlights. If desired,
   add a gold or bright red bow.
7. Hang the wreath outdoors for 12–24 hours in case the
   sphagnum moss is still dripping. When fully dry, hang
   indoors over the mantel, or on an outdoor or indoor wall.

Miniature Terrariums

As I gathered a basketful of tiny plants to make terrarium
Christmas balls, the pale winter sunshine made tromping
through the woods a pleasant adventure. Moss and small ferns
went into my basket along with slips of thyme I had gathered from the herb garden. My partridgeberry had no berries

on it so I decided to cheat a little and use some nandina berries instead.

A miniature forest captured in a glass ball, these tiny terrariums are as magical as a ship in a bottle. They look almost unbelievably delicate and are admittedly fragile, but will last for months and months with proper care. They must be planted through the neck of the ball, which usually only measures a half inch (1 cm) across. It may sound impossible, but it is really not that difficult if you are very careful in handling the extremely fragile glass balls. But count on losing one out of every five balls you make. Disaster can come from many directions. One year I dropped one on the doorstep of a friend as I was handing it to her. I inadvertently turned one upside down as I was hanging it in the window, turning my little forest into a mess of soil, pebbles, and plants. One broke as I was putting the pebbles in. Don't worry about it—just make a few extras.

A

B

TIME: 1 hour

COST: ☆

MATERIALS:

    7- or 9-inch (18- or 23-cm) diameter *clear* glass ornament balls (available at craft stores)

    1 tablespoon fine pebbles or gravel

    Pinch of charcoal (available from aquarium or pet stores)

    ⅓ cup (80 ml) potting soil

    Funnel

    Long tweezers, pencil, or chopstick

    Tiny leafed plants such as partridgeberry, thyme, or small ferns

    Moss

    Red berries

    Glue gun and glue, or white glue

    1 yard (1 m) ¼-inch (.7-cm) wide red satin ribbon

DIFFICULTY: ✂ ✂ ✂ ✂

SHELF LIFE: 1–6 months

1. Hold the glass ball gently but firmly in one hand, cupping your hand underneath the glass. Very slowly and very care- fully put the pebbles in the bottom of the ball first. Take a single pebble and slowly slide it into the ball. Do this again and again until you have covered the bottom of the ball with a thin layer of pebbles (photo A).

2. Using the funnel, sprinkle ½ teaspoon of charcoal over the pebbles. This will "sweeten" the soil and help prevent mold from growing.

3. Pour approximately ⅓ cup (80 ml) commercial potting soil through the funnel to the bottom of the ball. If the soil gets stuck in the mouth of the funnel, carefully use a pencil or chopstick to push it through. Keep adding soil until the ball is half full.

4. Remove the funnel and use the pencil to spread the soil evenly in the bottom of the ball. The soil should be at least ½ inch (1 cm) deep.

5. Start with the small plants. Pinch off 5–6 leaves *with roots attached* from the main clump. Ideally what you want is short, stocky, healthy roots with leaves growing as low on

the stem as possible. Fold this small plant division together, with the roots toward the bottom, and gently stuff it through the opening (photo B, page 116). Using the pencil, push the roots into the soil. Depending on the size of glass ball you are using and the size of your plants, try to plant 2–3 tiny clumps. Complete the planting by putting tiny pieces of moss around the plants.

6. If necessary, pour in a bit more potting soil to cover the roots of the plants.
7. Add 5 or 6 drops of water.
8. Drop in 3–4 red berries (Use partridge berries that are already attached to the plant if possible. If not, try nandina berries or holly berries—nandina lasts longer. The berries will not last as long as the rest of the plants but give the terrarium a festive air.)
9. Using a glue gun or white glue, spread a thin layer of glue around the neck of the ball. Carefully replace the top of the ball and allow to dry thoroughly.
10. Tie a ribbon around the top and hang in the window (photo C). The plants will grow quickly if they receive good sunlight or heat from a furnace vent. These balls also look magical when hung on the Christmas tree.

C

Variation: This does not have to be a Christmas craft. After Christmas I simply changed the red ribbon for fishing line and left seven of these hanging in my kitchen window in place of a curtain. This forest in a ball makes an unusual and wonderful gift.

Rose and Boxwood Topiary

There will be fourteen of us for Christmas dinner at my house, so I want the table to look particularly elegant. I decided to make a topiary tree out of boxwood and dried roses. Since I did not have enough dried red roses from my own garden, I supplemented them with store-bought dried white roses from my favorite craft store. The combination of red and white roses turned out to be beautiful.

When I had gathered as much boxwood as I dared from my own bushes, I went next door and offered to "prune" my neighbor's shrubs. She was delighted. So was I.

TIME: 2 hours
COST: ☆ to ☆☆☆ (depending on how many dried roses you have to buy)
MATERIALS:
  Small branch or stick about 14 inches (35 cm) long and at least 1 inch (3 cm) in diameter
  12-inch (30 cm) Styrofoam ball, either green or white
  Short boxwood branches (enough to fill a plastic kitchen garbage bag)
  24 dried roses
  Floral picks
  Floral tape
  14-inch (35-cm) clay pot
  Pebbles
  Potting soil
  Spanish or sphagnum moss
  1½ yards (1.3 m) ⅞-inch (2.2-cm) wide gold or red ribbon (wire-edged or stiff ribbon works best)
  Spray fixative (optional)
DIFFICULTY: ✄ ✄
SHELF LIFE: 4 weeks; longer if shellacked

1. Find a stick in the woods. The bark should be smooth and interesting. Cut or break to about 14 inches (35 cm) long. Sharpen one end to a slight point.
2. Push 5 or 6 inches (13 or 15 cm) of the pointed end of the stick into the Styrofoam ball until it is secure.
3. Prepare the clay pot by putting a generous layer of pebbles (3–4 inches [8–10 cm] deep) in the bottom. Fill the pot with potting soil, or continue to fill with pebbles.
4. Push the stick into the center of the prepared pot, through the soil and all the way down into the pebbles, making it as secure as possible. Add a bit of extra potting soil around the stick if necessary.
5. Cut short branches of boxwood approximately 2½–3 inches (6–8 cm) long. These should be as full as possible; forked branches work best since they fill space more quickly than single branches.
6. Insert the boxwood branches into the ball, close enough together to effectively cover the ball so that none of the Styrofoam shows through (photo A).
7. To give them extra strength, wire the roses to floral picks and snip off the long, fragile stems. Wrap the pick and the stem with floral tape so they will stay together as you insert them into the Styrofoam.
8. When you have covered a small area of the ball, insert a rose, making sure it stands out a bit from the boxwood (photo B). It's important to note that dried roses are delicate and can be tricky to get into the Styrofoam. Before inserting them into the ball make a hole in the Styrofoam with an empty pick where you want the rose to be. This will make it easier to put in the pick with the rose attached.
9. Continue to cover the ball with boxwood and roses, taking care to distribute the roses evenly throughout the boxwood.
10. Place handfuls of moss around the stick, effectively hiding the potting soil.

11. Tie the ribbon around the top of the pot or around the stick, and make a big bow on one side, allowing long pieces to trail over the pot or even onto the table.
12. Boxwood begins to dry out after 3 or 4 weeks. Spraying the entire thing with fixative will give it a shine and extend its life span by many weeks.

A

B

Basic Techniques

Pressing Flowers and Herbs

&

Pressing is fairly easy and takes few materials. The aim is to dry the plants as flat as possible; this can be done either in a commercially available plant press or in a heavy book.

Pick plant material at its prime. Do not try to use flowers that have already peaked; they will not hold up as well as those in good condition, since pressing will not improve them. Buds are also good to use, and leaves and foliage always give a nice balance.

Many different flowers lend themselves well to pressing. Those that do best are small, with thin plant parts. Look for nice plant forms where the leaf and flower parts stand out distinctly. More intricate forms such as those of daisies or cosmos are more attractive when pressed than such solid forms as peonies or hibiscus.

Place each plant part down flat on blotting paper. Arrange each piece into the appearance you want, because once they are dried they will be inflexible. Be sure to allow some material to curve and bend for a more natural look. Separate each plant piece so that it is not touching another piece. Cover with another piece of blotting paper and put in a press or between the pages of a book, or stack books on top of it.

The time needed for drying depends on the materials used. Some plants take only two or three days while others will take as much as three weeks to dry completely.

When arranging the flowers you can break off stems to rearrange to the height desired, or move leaves, substitute smaller ones, take out petals, or add others. "Painting" with pressed flowers is a versatile and easy craft.

Some plants are unsuitable for pressing because they lose their color too quickly. Spiderwort, for example, although thin and with a nice color and shape, is useless as a pressed flower because the pigment disappears so fast. Experiment with flowers from your own garden but be sure to press enough "tried and true" flowers (as listed below) to assure yourself of a good supply.

FOLIAGE

Artemisia · Clematis (stems) · Dusty miller · Ferns · Grass · Honeysuckle (stems and leaves) · Ivy · Maple leaves (small) · Queen Anne's lace

FLOWERS

SPRING: Carnation · Johnny-jump-up · Pansy · Phlox (wild blue) · Primrose · Scilla · Viola · Violet · Wallflower

SUMMER: Bachelor's buttons · Coreopsis (annual) · Cosmos · Daisy · Delphinium · Flax · Geranium · Impatiens · Larkspur · Nicotiana · Phlox · Roses (small flowers and buds) · Zinnia (single, not double varieties)

FALL: Aster · Calendula · Chrysanthemum (single variety) · Goldenrod · Hydrangea

WINTER: Christmas rose · Crocus · Winter jasmine

Wiring Flowers

❀

For strengthening, extending, or creating stems, it is useful to add thin wire to dried flowers. Wire is also used to keep small bunches of flowers together. A spool or precut lengths of fine florist wire are adequate for working with flowers.

To create or extend a stem, cut the flower head off, leaving at least an inch (3 cm) of stem attached. Lay the end of the wire alongside the piece of stem, overlapping as much as possible. Use floral tape to firmly secure the wire to the stem.

To strengthen a hollow stem, insert the wire up through the center of the stem.

Conditioning Fresh Flowers

❀

Whether fresh flowers from the garden are simply stuck in a glass jelly jar or elaborately arranged in a porcelain dish, they will last longer and look better if they are conditioned properly.

Some flowers, such as Christmas rose, must be conditioned or the stems will swoon and faint within a few hours of being picked. Conditioned properly, though, they will last many days.

Artemisia: Dip stems in boiling water for 20 seconds; leave in warm water for 2 hours.

Aster: Cut when three-quarters open and soak overnight in sugar solution. Lasts 6–10 days.

Calla lily leaves: Soak overnight in weak starch solution.

Chrysanthemum: Cut in full bloom, remove lower foliage, mash the ends of the stems with a hammer, and place in water to their necks for 3 hours or more.

Coreopsis: Cut blooms when fully open; place overnight in weak saline solution. Lasts 7–14 days.

Cosmos: Cut blooms when almost open; leave in cool water overnight. Lasts 5–8 days.

Dahlia: Dip stems in boiling water for 20 seconds; let stand in sugar solution that includes 1 aspirin. Lasts 5–7 days; smaller blossoms last longer.

Delphinium: Cut blooms when tops are still in bud; fill stem with weak starch solution and plug end with cotton. Lasts 7 days.

Gladiolus: Cut when buds begin to show color; set in cool water until ready to use.

Hosta leaves: Dip leaves in boiling water; submerge in cold water overnight.

Iris: Give a long drink before arranging. Lasts 7–10 days.

Lily: Bruises easily, so handle gently. Cut stems on a slant; place in warm water for several hours. Lasts 7 days.

Marigold: Scrape bottom of stem to expose inner tissue; remove foliage below water line. Lasts 7 days.

Narcissus: Cut as buds show color; wipe off sap before arranging stems in shallow water. Lasts 7 days.

Phlox: Cut when clusters are half open; split stems and soak overnight in cool water.

Peony: Cut when petals begin to open; put in warm water. Lasts 7 days.

Poppy: Cut before fully open; dip stems in boiling water for 20 seconds then place in cool water for several hours.

Primrose: Prick stems just under flower head; plunge into warm water for several hours.

Rose: Cut as buds begin to open; hammer stems. Lasts 5–7 days.

Sweet pea: Handle as little as possible. Arrange in shallow water. Lasts 7 days.

Tulip: Cut off white part of stem; prick stems just under flower head with a pin; wrap stems together in bunches in newspaper; place in a warm, weak starch solution.

Zinnia: Cut right above a leaf joint; remove extra foliage; place ends in boiling water for 20 seconds and then place in warm water for several hours.

Drying Flowers and Herbs

When picked and dried properly, certain flowers will last season after season. Many flowers can be dried by various methods—air drying, microwaving, or drying with a desiccant such as silica gel—and elaborate recipes exist for removing the moisture from everything from pansies to petunias. Many people get wonderful results and can make beautiful designer arrangements that look good enough to be in a museum.

But in drying flowers, as in any other kind of craft, the easier the better, and you will have better success in your crafts if you use flowers that dry naturally. Some of these you can grow in your garden; others can be easily and safely picked from the roadside. Keep your eyes open during the summer for interesting grasses and seed heads, which can be used for many wonderful crafts.

The oldest and still the easiest method for drying plants is air drying. It produces slightly muted colors, nice for most old-fashioned crafts. Air drying is easy if a few basic rules are followed. First, choose flowers that dry well. Some will shatter and others will shrivel up, but many retain their shape and color quite well. Second, pick the flowers while they are still in good condition. Some flowers do best when picked fully opened; others should be left on the stalk to dry.

Once you have picked the flowers, strip all the leaves off the stalk. The less plant material there is, the quicker the flowers will dry. Tie the flowering stalks in bunches of eight to ten and secure with string or a rubber band. Hang the bunches upside down, pinned to a clothesline or a beam in a dark area with good air circulation. An attic is often excellent for this, a basement rarely so. As long as the air is dry, though, and there is adequate ventilation, many different places will be suitable. Most air-dried flowers should be ready to use in ten to fourteen days.

Some flowers simply do not dry satisfactorily by this method. Fully opened roses, for example, will end up a bunch of petals on the floor. For heavier flowers, such as roses and zinnias, drying with a desiccant might be more desirable.

Flowers buried in a desiccant such as silica gel usually dry in two to seven days. To dry flowers in a powder such as this, cut off the blossom below the flower head and create a wire stem by poking a piece of florist's wire up through the blossom. Place a thin layer of powder in a wide, airtight container and place flowers in a single layer on top of the powder. Do not allow the petals to touch each other if you can help it. Carefully pour more powder into the container to cover the flowers completely, and close the lid tightly.

FLOWERS TO AIR-DRY

Baby's breath (pick when flowers start to dry)
Chive flowers (pick when fully open)
Cockscomb (pick flower heads when fully open)
Globe amaranth (leave on stem until very dry but pick before seeds begin to form)
Goldenrod (pick before fully open)
Hydrangea (leave on stem until flowers are crispy dry but harvest before they begin to turn brown)
Larkspur (best dried upright, with stems in 3 inches [8 cm] of water)
Lavender (pick just as buds are beginning to open)
Statice (pick when flowers begin to dry on stem)
Strawflower (pick before fully open)
Tansy (leave on stalk until very dry)
Yarrow (leave on stalk until very dry; yellow dries best)

Ten Best Dried Garden Flowers

Baby's breath	Lavender
Cockscomb	Rosebuds
Globe amaranth	Statice
Hydrangea	Strawflower
Larkspur	Yarrow

Tying the Perfect Bow

Making a bow is not as difficult as it may first appear. The basic concept is to create seven or eight loops of ribbon the same size, secure them in the center with thin wire, a piece of chenille, or a pipe cleaner, and then fluff out the loops on all sides to make a full, even bow. This type of bow can be purchased at nearly any good craft store, particularly during the holidays, but it is much less expensive and more fun to make your own. Besides, the bows you create can run the gamut from calico to brocade, limited only by the kinds of ribbon you can find.

A good-sized bow will take about 2½ yards (2 m) of ribbon, with an extra yard (m) or so for tails or streamers if you wish. You will also need lightweight wire or a chenille strip in a matching color.

1. Hold the ribbon with your thumb and forefinger so that about 5 inches (13 cm) sticks out above your thumb, right side of the ribbon facing you.
2. Make a 5-inch (13-cm) loop downward, keeping the right side facing you, pinch in, and hold with your thumb and finger, and make a 5-inch (13-cm) loop upward.
3. Keep making even loops above and beneath your thumb and finger until you have made a total of eight.

4. Take a piece of lightweight wire, a chenille strip, or a pipe cleaner and twist it tightly where your thumb and finger were holding the ribbon together.
5. Spread out the loops on all sides so that they are even and full. Add streamers if desired.

Making Jelly

One of the most beautiful ways to capture a honey-golden afternoon in the garden is to whip up a batch of sweet-flavored jelly. You can make jelly out of a wide assortment of ingredients, from traditional jelly plants such as blackberry and strawberry to more unusual and exotic plants such as kudzu, dandelion, and violet.

Jelly making is not nearly as difficult as you might think. You basically need juice extracted from berries or flowers, sugar, a fruit pectin (commercially available as Sure-Jell), a big pot, and jelly jars to put it all in.

Extracting the Juice

1. Work with relatively small amounts of berries or flowers at a time, 3–4 cups (750 ml–1 liter). Wash them thoroughly and place in a large, flat-bottomed pan; barely cover plant material with water.
2. Bring to a boil and then simmer until juice has been extracted from material. This can take anywhere from 5 to 45 minutes, depending on the material used. Often you can tell when all the good stuff has been extracted because the plant material will be almost colorless.
3. Take pan off stove and remove plant material. For crystal-clear jelly, put the contents of the pan into a "jelly bag" made from cheesecloth and allow the clear juice to drip into

a container. If you don't mind a few seeds and a little pulp, simply strain the juice using a wire strainer.

4. Measure the juice.

MAKING THE JELLY

For best results, you will need a large kettle with a broad, flat bottom, which allows the juice and sugar to boil quickly and evenly.

In general, you should add one cup (250 ml) of sugar for every cup (250 ml) of juice you have, and add one package powdered fruit pectin (1¾ ounces; 49 g) for every 3–4 cups (750 ml–1 liter) of juice.

Work in small quantities so that the jelly will set correctly.

1. Put measured juice into a 6–8-quart (1.5–2 liters) saucepan (but no more than 4 cups [1 liter] at a time).
2. Measure sugar into a separate bowl.

3. Add one package (49 g) of fruit pectin to the juice and bring to full boil. Add ½ teaspoon of margarine to keep juice from foaming.
4. Add the sugar all at once, allowing the mixture to return to a full boil. Boil for one minute, stirring constantly.

SEALING THE JARS

1. Fill hot, clean jars to ⅛ inch (.3 cm) of top. Cover with flat lids, screw on bands, and place in a hot-water bath. Make sure all jars are covered with hot water. Bring the water to a boil, and boil the jars for 10 minutes.
2. Remove the jars from the hot water and turn them upside down on a dish towel on counter. After one hour, check to make sure the jars have sealed. If sealed properly, the flat top will not move at all when pressed. If jars did not seal, either reprocess or store in refrigerator.

Creating a Crafts Garden

Ideas for a "Useful" Garden

&

People create gardens for a multitude of different reasons—for beauty, for food, for fragrance, to name just a few. If you love to make gifts from flowers and herbs, one of the best reasons to have a garden is to be able to use your own produce, eliminating the need to purchase materials for various crafts.

Unless you have plenty of resources, time, space, and sun, you probably won't be able to cultivate everything you require for these crafts. However, you should be able to grow most of what you need.

What you choose to plant in your garden depends on the materials you need for your favorite crafts, and on what you can grow well. In determining what you want to include in

your garden, first decide which crafts you are most likely to do, then make a list of the plants needed. You'll probably be surprised to learn that a few choice selections of herbs and flowers will supply you with much bounty.

Don't waste your time trying to grow plants that do not do well in your geographic area. Although I love dried baby's breath, I simply don't have success with it where I live; our soils are much too acidic. So I use that spot in my garden to grow something that flourishes. I usually make crafts from what I have the most of. I do a lot with thyme, rosemary, and lemon balm because they all grow so abundantly in my garden. I also rely on forget-me-nots in spring crafts because the conditions in my garden are just right for growing this little blue flower. I always have baskets full.

Do I "use" everything in my garden? Of course not. I grow lilies because they are beautiful, and I don't pick them to bring inside. I'm happy just to have them in the garden. But before I put in a new plant, I do think about its usefulness. Very often you can choose a plant that is both beautiful and practical.

Your crafts garden will be a mixture of plants that will include some long-term plants such as apple trees, holly, juniper, and boxwood; perennial flowers such as roses, daisies, yarrow, and bee balm; perennial herbs such as rosemary, thyme, sage, and mint; annual flowers such as statice, Johnny-jump-ups, and zinnias; and annual herbs such as basil and parsley.

The ingredients for a garden are few and simple. Basically, you need water, sunshine, soil, and plants. The shape, size, and composition of your garden will depend on your own resources and the amount of time and energy you want to put into it. My own garden is composed of a hillside planted with a mixture of perennials, annuals, and flowering shrubs, and a series of terraced beds where I grow my herbs and other flowers.

The limiting factor in my garden is sunshine. I'm surrounded by trees that I just can't bear to cut down, even to grow more beautiful and prolific flowers, so I grow what I can. Even so, ignoring the lessons of seasons past, I continually plant species that really need more sun and hope that they will miraculously do better than last year.

Starting Out

&

Before you dig the first shovelful of dirt, you have some work to do. You need to be knowledgeable about your garden spot so that you can make the best use of the resources that you have. When you are considering a site for your garden:

1. Determine the number of full-sun hours the site receives.
2. Determine the fertility and composition of the soil by having a soil analysis performed at the county extension service.
3. Determine how you will get water to the site in case Mother Nature does not cooperate.

SUN

You can make a garden in an area that does not receive much sun, but you will be severely limited in what you can grow well. Many of the books and instructions will say certain plants "tolerate shade," but remember that there is a big difference between tolerance and abundance. I can't grow abundant roses, but I can grow tolerable roses and I continue to do so because they supply me with enough petals and buds to do many crafts.

I take advantage of small areas that receive pockets of sunshine, and here I plant those species that need the most sun: globe amaranth, statice, zinnias, and the like. In the corner that rarely sees more than a few filtered rays of sun, I grow my ferns, which thrive in the shade.

SOIL

Most county extension services offer soil-analysis testing. This is an invaluable tool to let you know what you're planting in and how you can work to improve it. Almost all soils benefit from the addition of organic matter, such as well-rotted compost. Amend your soil as necessary and you'll be well rewarded.

WATER

The amount of water you must supply to the garden depends on how much rainfall your area gets and on the types of plants that you use. If you live in a very dry area, adjust your plantings accordingly. Try growing water-loving species close to the water source, and more drought-tolerant plants farther away. Water is particularly critical when seedlings are small. Supply ample water until they have become well established.

Preparing the Site

&

Most people create a garden by making a series of beds. For a crafts garden they can be particularly useful because small beds allow for easy access and harvest.

When preparing new beds, it is necessary to dig down 18 inches (45 cm) to 2 feet (60 cm). It may seem ridiculous to dig 2 feet (60 cm) to plant a seed $\frac{1}{8}$ inch (.3 cm) long, but remember that that little seed will grow into a big plant with big roots. The easier it is for the roots to get through the soil, the happier your plants are going to be.

Amend the soil as necessary, adding compost, well-rotted manure, and other organic matter. If you think it absolutely essential to add chemical fertilizers, do so sparingly.

Selecting Plants

&

First make a list of all the plants you would like to grow in your garden, based on the kinds of crafts you want to do. Then do your homework by looking up these various plants to see if

they match the environmental conditions of your garden—sun, soil type, water availability, and so on. The list at the end of this chapter will give you good basic information about many of the plants needed for these crafts.

If you are a new gardener, talk to other gardeners in your region. Gardeners love to give advice and are not shy about telling you if certain flowers or vegetables are easy or difficult to grow in your area.

When you purchase plants, buy only the ones that look fresh and healthy. Don't try to save pennies by getting discount plants that look tired or have already wilted.

Get a good basic gardening book on your region (available at the library) and look up suggested planting dates for your particular area. Do not plant heat-loving annuals too soon in spring. A late frost can wreak havoc on a spring garden.

Planting Suggestions

Following is a basic list of flowers, vegetables, herbs, and shrubs to cultivate that will give you a wonderful supply of materials for most of the crafts in this book. This list includes only plants that are useful and easy to grow. Most are hardy enough to be grown easily in every horticultural zone.

Flowers

Artemisia · Baby's breath · Bachelor's buttons · Bloodroot · Cockscomb · Coreopsis · Cosmos · Crocus · Dahlia · Daisy · Dianthus · Ferns · Forget-me-not · Globe amaranth · Goldenrod · Impatiens · Lantana · Larkspur · Lavender · Lily of the valley · Marigold · Pansy · Peony · Phlox · Primrose · Rose · Statice · Strawflower · Sunflower · Yarrow · Zinnia

ARTEMISIA (*Artemisia ludoviciana*)

Description:	Attractive gray green foliage forms neat mounds 24–36 inches (60–90 cm) tall. Leaves are finely dissected and aromatic.
Cultivars:	'Silver King'
Type:	Perennial
Blooms:	Used only for foliage
Sun:	Full
Soil:	Well drained, not too rich
Water:	Sparingly
Comments:	Does not like excessive heat and humidity, and tends to rot without good air circulation. Considered hardy perennial where

summer temperatures are cool. If mildew becomes a problem, cut the plant back severely and new growth should be firm and healthy.

Harvest: Late summer or early fall

Uses: Pick long stems of foliage. Strip off the lower, blemished leaves, leaving the rest on the stem. Hang up to air-dry in small bundles. The leaves and stems will be very brittle and will need careful handling.

BABY'S BREATH *(Gypsophila paniculata)*

Description: A multibranched plant bearing many small white (sometimes pink) flowers and few leaves on thin, wiry stems. Height varies from 18 to 48 inches (45–120 cm).

Cultivars: 'Perfecta' has double white blossoms and grows 36 inches (90 cm) tall; 'Pink Fairy' has large double pink flowers and grows 18 inches (45 cm) tall.

Type: Perennial (annual type also available)

Blooms: Summer

Sun: Full

Soil: Alkaline

Water: Average

Comments: If your soil is too acidic, add ground limestone, or grow in a container with neutral soils.

Harvest: Any time during growing season

Uses: Fresh or dried

BACHELOR'S BUTTONS *(Centaurea cyanus)*

Description: Delicate, airy plants 24–36 inches (60–90 cm) high with bright blue, pink, red, or white blossoms.

Cultivars: 'Polka Dot' is a mixture of blue, pinks, and white; 'Jubilee Gem' is only 12–15 inches (30–38 cm) tall, with dwarf blue flowers.

Type: Annual

Blooms: Late spring and summer

Sun: Full

Soil: Well drained, not too rich

Water: Sparingly

Comments: Plants will flop over in too rich a soil or not enough sun, and may need to be staked. Withstands drought, tolerant of cold and even light frost. Grow in a sunny area with good air circulation. Not a long-lived plant, and will flower for only a few weeks.

Harvest: Early summer

Uses: Fresh or dried

BLOODROOT *(Sanguinaria canadensis)*

Description: Bright white blossoms with 7–16 petals on solitary stem. Leaves deeply lobed, heart-shaped, 8 inches (20 cm) across at maturity. Plant grows only 6–8 inches (15–20 cm) tall.

Type: Perennial

Blooms: Early spring

Sun: Dappled shade, filtered sun

Soil: Humus, rich

Water: Likes even moisture while in bloom

Comments: This is a native wildflower, found growing in woodland areas.

Harvest: Root only in summer or early fall

Uses: Root used for dye

COCKSCOMB *(Celosia agentea plumosa* and *C. a. cristata)*

Description: Flowers are either long plumes or flattened crests. Blossoms come in red, gold, and cream. Generally grows 18–24 inches (45–60 cm); dwarf species grow 12 inches (30 cm) tall.

Cultivars: 'Century' is a plume type of mixed colors, 20–24 inches (50–60 cm) tall; 'Apricot Brandy' has unusual orange plumes and is

COCKSCOMB *(continued)*

an early bloomer; 'Chief' is a crested type and is the best for cut and dried flowers because of its long stems.

Type:	Tender annual
Blooms:	Summer
Sun:	Full
Soil:	Average to rich, slightly acidic
Water:	Average to ample
Comments:	Though cockscomb will tolerate high temperatures, it is very sensitive to frost. Can be grown from seed. Do not transplant seedlings too deeply.
Harvest:	Any time during blooming season
Uses:	Dried or fresh

COREOPSIS *(Coreopsis tinctoria)*

Description:	Tall plant with long slender leaves. Blossoms measure 1 inch (3 cm) across and come in shades of yellow, gold, and maroon.
Cultivars:	None
Type:	Annual
Blooms:	Summer
Sun:	Full
Soil:	Dry, low in fertility, well drained
Water:	Sparse
Comments:	Coreopsis comes easily from seed and grows quickly.
Harvest:	Any time during blooming season
Uses:	Petals—fresh or pressed—are used to create a burnt orange or bright yellow dye.

COSMOS *(Cosmos bipinnatus* and *C. sulphureus)*

Description:	Pink or white cosmos *(C. bipinnatus)* grows 24–30 inches (60–75 cm) tall, with each blossom 4–5 inches (10–13 cm) across. *C. sulphureus* is shorter, producing red, orange, or yellow balls of flowers.
Cultivars:	There are many named cultivars for both species, all of which are suitable.
Type:	Annual
Blooms:	Summer
Sun:	Full, tolerates some shade in very hot areas
Soil:	Rich garden, neutral, well drained
Water:	Keep evenly moist but not wet
Comments:	Cosmos will tolerate high temperatures but is killed by frost. Comes easily from seed.
Harvest:	Throughout growing season
Uses:	*C. sulphureus*—fresh or pressed—is the source of red and yellow dye.

CROCUS *(Crocus sp.)*

Description:	Dutch crocus varieties are hybrids of many different species. These have large blossoms in white, yellow, and purple. Foliage is thin and grasslike; blossoms are cup-shaped. Plant height is 4–5 inches (10–13 cm).
Cultivars:	'Pickwick' has white petals with deep purple stripes and a bright yellow or orange stamen in the center; 'Yellow Mammoth' is golden yellow; 'Snow Storm' is stark white with a startlingly bright orange stamen.
Type:	Perennial (from bulb)
Blooms:	Early spring or fall
Sun:	Full sun or light shade
Soil:	Light, sandy, not too rich
Water:	Moderate
Comments:	Crocus bulbs should be planted only 3–4 inches (8–10 cm) deep, in early fall. After flowers bloom, do not cut the foliage but allow it to die back naturally.
Harvest:	Spring or fall—during peak of bloom.
Uses:	Dye from stigmas, pressed blossoms, and leaves; forced for indoor bloom; fresh, makes a good cut flower.

DAHLIA *(Dahlia sp.)*

Description: There are two main types of dahlias—anemone forms with softly cupped and rounded petals, and cactus forms with long, narrow spinelike petals. These come in yellow, orange, red, white, cream, pink, and maroon. Dwarf forms grow 12–18 inches (30–45 cm) tall, regular forms grow 24–60 inches (60–150 cm) tall.

Cultivars: Anemone forms: 'Fable'–scarlet, 30 inches (75 cm); 'Honey'–apricot and pink, 30 inches (75 cm); 'San Luis Rey'–pink, 48 inches (120 cm)

Cactus forms: 'Gold Crown'–bronze yellow; 'Brookside Cheri'–salmon pink, 48–60 inches (120–150 cm); 'Park Jewel'–dark pink, 24 inches (60 cm)

Type: Tender perennial
Blooms: Summer and early fall
Sun: Full
Soil: Rich, neutral, well drained
Water: Even moisture during growing season
Comments: Dahlias are grown from tubers. In frost-free areas they can be left in the ground throughout the year. In other areas the tubers should be dug before the first fall frost and stored indoors to be replanted in spring. Plant the tubers 6 inches (15 cm) deep when all danger of frost has passed in spring.
Harvest: Any time during growing season
Uses: Yellow and orange varieties of the cut flower produce a yellow dye.

DAISY *(Chrysanthemum leucanthemum)*

Description: Bright white ray flowers surround a yellow center; leaves are dark green with wavy edges; plant usually grows 12–24 inches (30–60 cm) tall. Although Shasta daisy cultivars are more beautiful garden flowers, it is the plain species that will be most useful for crafts, with the added advantage of being easier to grow.

Cultivars: None
Type: Short-lived perennial
Blooms: Late spring and early summer
Sun: Full
Soil: Moderately rich
Water: Sparingly; will withstand dry conditions
Comments: Ox-eye daisy comes easily from seed but will not bloom until the second year.
Harvest: Before flowers begin to fade
Uses: Choose perfect, small blooms for pressed flowers; also used as a cut flower.

DIANTHUS *(Dianthus plumarius)*

Description: Spicy scented flowers in shades of pink, red, and white, sometimes yellow. Foliage is long, slender, and grasslike. In some species the leaves are light gray green.

Cultivars: 'Spring Beauty' is a mixture of double flowers in shades of pink, rose, salmon, and white. 'Essex Witch' is a rose pink dwarf

DIANTHUS *(continued)*

variety only 5 inches (13 cm) tall. 'Aqua' has white double flowers on stalks 10–12 inches (25–30 cm) tall.

Type:	Perennial
Blooms:	Spring and summer
Sun:	Full
Soil:	Rich, well drained
Water:	Average to moist
Comments:	Dianthus can be propagated by cuttings or divisions.
Harvest:	Any time plants are in bloom
Uses:	Petals or entire flowers are dried for potpourri; red varieties can be pressed to an attractive muted dark red color; also used as a cut flower.

FERNS

Description:	Many species of ferns can be grown in the home garden: *Dryopteris ludoviciana*—Louisiana shield fern; *Adiantum pedatum*—American maidenhair fern, wonderful light green, with delicate fronds; *Osmunda cinnamomea*—cinnamon fern, tall, graceful, with cinnamon-colored spires in spring; *Polystichum acrostichiodes*—Christmas fern, perhaps the most common and the easiest to grow.
Type:	Perennial
Sun:	Shade to partial shade
Soil:	Rich, loamy
Water:	Even moisture
Comments:	Ferns should be transplanted from nursery grown plants and not dug from the wild.
Harvest:	Summer–fall
Uses:	Do not cut immature fronds as they do not last well in water; pressed fronds are more satisfactory than fresh or dried ferns.

FORGET-ME-NOT *(Myosotis scorpioides semperflorens)*

Description:	Dainty blue flowers with yellow eyes form neat, low-growing mounds. The attractive foliage is bright green, turning bronzy after the flowers bloom.
Cultivars:	None
Type:	Perennial
Blooms:	April–May (some types bloom well into summer)
Sun:	Partial shade
Soil:	Rich
Water:	Moist
Harvest:	Gather when most flowers are opened along the stalk; do not wait too long.
Uses:	For pressed flowers, turn small flowers face up, not to the side.

GLOBE AMARANTH *(Gomphrena globosa)*

Description:	The cloverlike, papery flower heads come in shades of purple, lavender, white, pink, orange, and yellow; can grow to 30 inches (75 cm) tall.
Cultivars:	'Strawberry Fields' is a deep, rich red color; other cultivars often come in mixtures of pinks and purples.
Type:	Annual
Sun:	Full
Soil:	Light, well drained, not too rich
Water:	Drought-resistant
Harvest:	Pick as flower heads are just opening
Uses:	Cut flowers last several days in water; also used dried and for seeds.

GOLDENROD *(Solidago sp.)*

Description:	Heights range from 1 to 5 feet (30–150 cm). Plants have plumes of bright yellow flowers; leaves are long and narrow.
Cultivars and species:	Among the best for crafts are *S. rugosa,* rough-leaved; *S. sempervirens,* seaside; and *S. odora,* scented.
Type:	Perennial
Blooms:	Late summer–fall
Sun:	Full
Soil:	Withstands average to poor soils
Water:	Drought-tolerant
Comments:	If you don't have room in your garden for these plants, they can often be found along the roadside, but ask permission before picking. Contrary to popular belief, goldenrod does not cause hay fever.
Harvest:	Gather flowers before they open fully.
Uses:	Goldenrod can be used cut, dried, or for dye.

IMPATIENS *(Impatiens wallerana)*

Description:	A very popular summer garden plant, impatiens come in many different shades including pink, red, orange, tangerine, white, and violet. Flowers are very thin, measure 1–2 inches (3–5 cm) across and appear in great profusion. Stems are weak and are easily broken.
Cultivars:	'Accent' grows only 6–8 inches (15–20 cm) tall; 'Blitz' has relatively large blossoms, 2½ inches (6 cm) across; 'Super Elfin' is often considered best all-round bloomer.
Type:	Annual
Sun:	Full, or partial shade
Water:	Ample
Harvest:	Fully opened blossoms
Uses:	Pressed flowers

LANTANA *(Lantana camara)*

Description:	Common lantana is a perennial shrub in frost-free areas but is used as an annual in other regions. It can grow as tall as 4 feet (1.2 m), though some species trail rather than grow upright. Flowers are bright and come in shades of yellow, orange, pink, or white.
Cultivars and species:	*L. montevidensis,* weeping lantana, is a trailing species that has weak, vinelike stems growing 3 feet (1 m) long. Blossoms are pink or lilac.
Type:	Tender perennial, often treated as an annual
Sun:	Full
Water:	Light, dry soil preferred
Harvest:	Fully opened flowers
Uses:	Fresh flowers used in bouquets, tussie-mussies; also pressed.

LARKSPUR *(Consolida ambigua)*

Description:	Tall spires of purple, blue, or pink flowers grow 2–5 feet (60–150 cm).
Type:	Annual
Sun:	Full
Soil:	Rich, loose, slightly alkaline
Water:	Ample
Comments:	Blooms best in late spring before summer temperatures get too hot

LARKSPUR *(continued)*

Harvest: Any time during blooming season

Uses: Used as a cut flower, or dried in stalks.

LAVENDER, ENGLISH *(Lavandula angustifolia)*

Description: Long spires of purple flowers above gray green leaves.

Cultivars: English lavender has the sweetest scent and is the species most often used in sachets, potpourri, and soap. 'Munstead' has dark purple flowers; 'Jean Davis' has white blossoms tinged with pink.

Type: Perennial

Blooms: Late spring–summer

Sun: Full

Soil: Rich, very well drained

Water: Relatively dry

Comments: English lavender is difficult to grow in hot, humid conditions. As an alternative, try French or Spanish lavender.

Harvest: Leaves and flowers any time during blooming season

Uses: Lavender is used cut, dried, in potpourri, and in scented oils and waters.

LILY OF THE VALLEY *(Convallaria majalis)*

Description: The arching flower stalks have 10–15 small, fragrant, bell-shaped blossoms; leaves are dark green and ribbed.

Cultivars: 'Giant Bells' sports 15 large flowers.

Type: Perennial (from small pips)

Sun: Light shade, filtered sunlight

Soil: Rich, well drained

Water: Water during very dry spells

Harvest: Leaves should be harvested during spring, summer, or early fall; flowers, any time in bloom.

Comments: Lily of the valley benefits from a fall side dressing of well-rotted compost.

Uses: Used as a cut or pressed flower; leaves used for dye; dried flowers for fragrance in potpourri.

MARIGOLD *(Tagetes patula)*

Description: Different species range in height from 6 to 36 inches (15–90 cm). Flowers, either single or double, come in shades of yellow, orange, dark red, and white.

Type: Annual

Sun: Full

Soil: Moderately rich

Water: Ample moisture

Harvest: Any time during growing season; harvest seeds when seed head is dry and brittle.

Uses: Flowers are edible—use chopped up in egg and cheese dishes; other uses are fresh cut flowers and dried in potpourri; seeds are good for collecting.

PANSY *(Viola wittrockiana)*

Description: Flowers, borne on separate stems, come in many different colors including blue, purple, yellow, orange, red, white, and bicolor.

Cultivars: 'Crystal Bowl' has 2½-inch (6 cm) blooms with no markings; 'Majestic Giant' has large, 4-inch (10 cm) blooms.

Type: Annual

Sun: Full sun or partial shade

Soil: Rich, high in organic matter

Water: Moist

Comments: In a mild climate, pansies can be set out in late summer or early fall. They like cool temperatures and will bolt during summer.

Uses: Use fresh or pressed, or dried in potpourri;

the edible flowers can be put in salads, jams, and jellies.

PEONY *(Paeonia officinalis)*

Description:	Common peony grows 2–4 feet (60–120 cm) tall and has large 3–6-inch (8–15 cm) blossoms in white, pink, or red. Single flowers have one row of petals; double and semi-double flowers have many rows of petals, creating a full blossom head. Leaves are large and remain attractive throughout spring and summer.
Cultivars:	'Miss America' has snow white petals, attractive golden stamen; 'Dinner Plate' is a clear pink; 'Gay Paree' has vibrantly colored pink petals on the outside, variegated pink and white petals on the inside.
Type:	Perennial
Sun:	Full
Water:	Generous, water during dry spells
Harvest:	Buds should be picked just as they begin to loosen; pick flowers before they are fully opened.
Uses:	Dried flowers, petals in potpourri

PHLOX *(Phlox paniculata)*

Description:	Summer phlox are tall (2–3 feet; 60–90 cm), sweet-smelling flowers that come in a variety of colors. Flower heads are attractive mounds of five-petaled florets.
Cultivars:	'White Admiral'—white; 'Bright Eyes'—light pink with dark pink centers; 'Vintage Wine'—claret red, blooms late in summer; 'Blue Lagoon'—large lavender-blue flowers.
Type:	Perennial
Sun:	Full
Water:	Moderate
Comments:	Phlox are prone to mildew. To guard against it, water at the base of the plant and do not wet the leaves and blossoms.
Harvest:	Pick blossoms in full bloom.
Uses:	Cut or pressed

PRIMROSE *(Primula veris)*

Description:	Bright or pale yellow flowers occur in whorls above thick, crinkly leaves.
Type:	Perennial
Sun:	Partial shade
Soil:	Rich, high in organic matter
Water:	Even moisture
Harvest:	As flowers are beginning to open
Uses:	Pressed or fresh-cut

ROSE *(Rosa sp.)*

Description:	Hybrid tea roses have large blossoms on long stems; floribundas have smaller blossoms borne in clusters; modern shrubs offer large flowers; climbers and ramblers display vigorous climbing habits and smaller flowers.
Type:	Perennial
Sun:	Full
Soil:	Very rich, loose soils with neutral pH
Water:	Constant, even moisture
Comments:	Roses take a good bit of care, but no flower is more valuable to the crafty gardener than the rose. The beds should be dug 1 foot

ROSE *(continued)*

(30 cm) deep and allowed to settle before plants are put in. They need to be fertilized regularly, checked for pests on a regular basis, and pruned in late winter. Old-fashioned roses often have the best fragrance.

Harvest: Gather buds and opened flowers throughout spring and summer; petals as the flowers begin to shatter; and rose hips.

Uses: Buds can be used fresh or dried; opened blossoms are beautiful as cut flowers; petals are used for making potpourri, rose water, and essential oil; hips for jams and jellies.

STATICE *(Limonium sinuatum)*

Description: A 24-inch (60 cm) tall, multibranched plant that has sprays of papery flowers in yellow, purple, blue, or rose

Type: Annual

Sun: Full

Soil: Rich, well drained

Water: Even moisture

Comments: Too much moisture causes the flowers to turn brown and fall off the stem.

Harvest: Harvest flowers when fully opened, seeds when heads are brittle.

Uses: Fresh-cut, dried, or for seeds

STRAWFLOWER *(Helichrysum bracteatum)*

Description: Strawflower is an everlasting plant that thrives in hot weather. The blossoms are small and daisylike with pointed petals. Colors include white, yellow, pink, deep rose, orange, red, and magenta.

Cultivars and species: 'Bright Bikini' has flowers 2 inches (5 cm) wide and grows about 12 inches (30 cm) tall. *Monstrosum* grows 20–30 inches (50–75 cm) tall and comes in all colors.

Type: Annual or tender perennial

Sun: Full

Water: Average to low

Harvest: Flowers in full bloom

Uses: Excellent dried flower

SUNFLOWER *(Helianthus annuus)*

Description: Huge, bright yellow blossom with dark center; can grow very tall.

Cultivars: 'Russian Giant' has a very large blossom and is good for collecting seeds; grows 8 feet (2 m) tall; 'Sunspot' has a big flower on a plant only 18 inches (45 cm) tall.

Type: Annual

Sun: Full

Soil: Tolerates dry, infertile soil

Water: Needs little water

Comments: Do not fertilize or overwater; may need staking.

Uses: Hulled seeds are used for snacks, unhulled seeds for bird food.

YARROW *(Achillea filipendulina)*

Description: Yarrow produces flat clusters of yellow flowers; leaves are dark green and finely dissected.

Cultivars: 'Gold Plate' is a mustard color, 3–4 feet (90–120 cm) tall; 'Coronation Gold' has bright yellow flowers and is 4 feet (120 cm) tall.

Type: Perennial

Sun: Full

Soil: Poor to average, moderately well drained

Water: Established plants are drought-tolerant.

Comments: Other yarrow species come in white, pink, or red.

Uses: Flowers are used dried, leaves can be pressed or used for tea.

ZINNIA (*Zinnia elegans*)

Description:	The three main types of zinnias are the dahlia type, cactus type, and bedding type. Zinnias bloom in every color except blue; height ranges from 6 to 36 inches (15–90 cm).
Cultivars and species:	'Cut and Come Again' makes a good cut flower; 'Rose Pinwheel' has pretty pink flowers that dry well; *Z. angustifolia* has single orange flowers good for pressing.
Type:	Annual
Sun:	Full
Soil:	Rich in organic matter, well drained
Water:	Average to moist
Uses:	Cut; some species are good for pressing, drying, and dyes.

Herbs

> Basil · Bay · Bee balm · Catnip · Chamomile, Roman · Lemon balm · Mint · Oregano · Parsley · Rosemary · Tarragon · Thyme

BASIL (*Ocimum basilicum*)

Description:	Shrublike plant is 1–2 feet (30–60 cm) tall, with fleshy, aromatic leaves and small white flowers.
Cultivars and species:	*O. americanum,* lemon basil, has a nice lemon fragrance and is good in vinegar; 'Nano Compatto Vero' has good texture and flavor; 'Purpurascens' is very ornamental with deep purple shiny leaves and is good as garnish and in vinegar.
Type:	Annuals or tender perennials
Sun:	Full
Soil:	Rich, moist, well drained
Water:	Moderate
Uses:	Leaves are used for pesto sauce, as vinegar flavoring, and in salsa and tomato sauce. They are best when used fresh, but can also be dried or frozen.

BAY (*Laurus nobilis*)

Description:	This evergreen shrub has shiny, unnotched leaves 1½–3½ inches (4–9 cm) long. It can grow to 5 feet (1.5 m) when planted in container, and up to 10 feet (3 m) in the garden.
Type:	Perennial
Sun:	Full
Soil:	Rich, well drained, slightly acidic
Water:	Moderate
Comments:	Susceptible to cold; must be brought indoors during winter months where temperatures dip well below freezing
Harvest:	Collect leaves sparingly at beginning of season, more aggressively toward end of season.
Comments:	Before frost hits, pot up to bring indoors; should last 2–3 months.
Uses:	Use dried leaves for culinary flavoring and as decoration in strings of beans and peppers, in wreaths, and in arrangements.

BEE BALM (*Monarda didyma*)

Description:	This tall plant has large pinkish red flowers appearing in whorls, square stems, and fuzzy leaves. It flowers in July and August.
Cultivars:	'Alba' has ivory blooms; 'Mahogany' has deep red flowers.
Type:	Perennial
Sun:	Full sun to partial shade
Soil:	Moist, rich in organic material
Water:	Moderate moisture

| Harvest: | Collect leaves just before plant blooms and again toward the end of blooming season. |
| Uses: | Bee balm makes excellent herbal tea; dried leaves are used in potpourri; leaves and blossoms are used as garnish. |

CATNIP *(Nepeta cataria)*

Description:	A member of the mint family, catnip has square stems and opposite leaves that are gray green above and whitish below. The light purple flowers are small and tubular and bloom mid to late summer. The plant is low-growing (1–3 feet [30–90 cm] tall) and spreads rapidly.
Type:	Perennial
Sun:	Full to partial shade
Soil:	Sandy, well drained, neutral pH
Water:	Average
Harvest:	Any time during growing season
Uses:	Dried or fresh leaves are used for tea, dried leaves for catnip bags, and dried leaves and flowers in potpourri or as an addition to bath bags.

CHAMOMILE, ROMAN *(Chamaemelum nobile)*

Description:	Low-growing with small, daisylike white flowers and soft, threadlike leaves, chamomile blooms late spring through late summer.
Cultivars and species:	German chamomile *(Matricaria recutita),* a hardy annual that grows 2–3 feet (60–90 cm) tall, is very similar to Roman chamomile.
Type:	Perennial
Sun:	Full
Soil:	Dry, sandy
Water:	Sparingly
Harvest:	Any time during blooming season
Uses:	Dried leaves and petals are used for tea; dried flowers are used for bath bags, potpourri, steam baths, and facial lotions.

LEMON BALM *(Melissa officinalis)*

Description:	Lemon balm has thick, crinkly, highly aromatic leaves, grows to 2 feet (60 cm) high, and produces small white flowers from July to September.
Type:	Perennial
Sun:	Full, to partial shade
Soil:	Neutral pH, sandy, well drained
Water:	Moderate
Harvest:	Early spring–fall
Uses:	Dried leaves are used in potpourri, scented hot pads, and bath bags.

MINT *(Mentha sp.)*

Description:	Mint features square stems, small tubular flowers, opposite aromatic leaves, and spreading rootstock, and grows to 2 feet (60 cm) tall.
Cultivars and species:	Dozens of varieties are available, including curly, spearmint, peppermint, apple mint, and pineapple mint.
Type:	Perennial
Sun:	Full to partial shade
Soil:	Slightly acidic, rich, well drained
Water:	Prefers moist conditions
Comments:	Many kinds of mint can become quite invasive, so handle with care.
Harvest:	Any time during growing season
Uses:	Fresh or dried leaves are used in tea, dried leaves in bath bags and scented hot pads.

OREGANO *(Origanum herocleoticum)*

| Description: | With small leaves and clusters of flowers, the entire plant 18 to 36 inches (45–90 cm) tall. |

OREGANO (continued)

Cultivars and species:	Another species that is highly flavorful is Mexican or Puerto Rican oregano, a member of the verbena family.
Type:	Perennial
Sun:	Full
Water:	Moderate
Harvest:	Small leaves during summer
Uses:	Good for drying or using fresh in soup, stews, and sauces.

PARSLEY *(Petroselinum crispum)*

Description:	Parsley has bright green pungent leaves and grows 1½ feet (45 cm) tall.
Cultivars and varieties:	Italian parsley, with large, flat, toothed leaves, has superior flavor. Curly-leaf parsley has crinkly, ruffled leaves and is highly ornamental.
Type:	Biennial
Sun:	Full
Soil:	Slightly acidic, moderately rich, well drained
Water:	Ample
Comments:	Very high in vitamins A and C, calcium, and iron
Harvest:	Gather sparingly at beginning of summer, more later in the season.
Uses:	Fresh or dried in cooking; fresh in salsa, pesto, and as a garnish

ROSEMARY *(Rosmarinus officinalis)*

Description:	This attractive evergreen shrub has needle-like leaves and grows 5–6 feet (1.5–1.8 m) tall outdoors. Pale blue flowers appear in early summer.
Cultivars:	'Miss Jessup' has golden green foliage; var. *prostratus* has long twisting branches.
Type:	Tender perennial

Sun:	Full to partial shade
Soil:	Sandy, loose, well drained, neutral pH
Water:	Moderate
Comments:	Must be brought indoors during harsh winter months.
Harvest:	Any time during growing season; do not harvest more than one third of the plant at a time.
Uses:	Potted rosemary is good for topiary; fresh for flavoring; dried for hair rinse, bath bags, scented hot pads, potpourri, Christmas sachets, tied in bundles for barbecue, woven into baskets, or as flavoring in vinegar and oil.

TARRAGON *(Artemisia dracunculus)*

Description:	Grows 2 feet (60 cm) tall. Leaves are linear, 1–4 inches (3–10 cm) long, unnotched on edges.
Cultivars:	Fresh tarragon, var. *sativa,* is highly aromatic, good for flavoring; Russian tarragon lacks fragrance and flavor so is of limited usefulness.
Type:	Perennial
Sun:	Full to partial shade
Soil:	Neutral, sandy, well drained
Water:	Sparingly
Comments:	Tarragon is difficult to grow in humid, damp conditions.
Harvest:	Any time during growing season
Uses:	Excellent fresh for flavoring vinegars and salads, or for garnishes. The flavor of frozen tarragon is superior to that of dried.

THYME *(Thymus vulgaris)*

Description:	The many different varieties have small oval leaves on woody stems and may grow

1 foot (30 cm) tall. Tubular blossoms are numerous, lavender to pink.

Cultivars and species: *T.* × *citriodorus* (lemon thyme) grows 4–12 inches (10–30 cm) and has yellow-edged leaves and a distinct lemon scent; *T. Herba-barona* (caraway thyme) has a caraway scent and provides good ground cover; *T. praecox arcticus* (mother of thyme) grows only 4 inches (10 cm) tall and forms a thick mat with rose-colored blossoms.

Type: Perennial

Sun: Full to partial shade

Soil: Slightly acidic, light, well drained

Water: Average

Harvest: Gather throughout the year in mild climates, spring–fall in the north

Uses: Fresh as flavoring in cooking or woven into baskets; dried for bath bags, in potpourri, or for cooking

Vegetables

Corn · Gourds · Onion · Peppers

CORN (*Zea mays rugosa*)

Description: This grassy plant grows to 9 feet (3 m) tall and produces ears of white, yellow, or bicolored kernels in papery husks.

Cultivars and varieties: Field corn, grown for animal food, has much wider shucks, making it superior for corn-shuck dolls.

Type: Annual

Sun: Full

Soil: Rich, well drained

Water: Ample

Comments: Any of the bright yellow corns will dry well for stringing. Use field corn for shucks.

Harvest: Collect fruit and shucks in summer.

Uses: Shucks for corn-shuck dolls; yellow cobs for dried corn.

GOURDS

Description: Gourds are bizarre-looking, inedible vegetables with no scent. They come in odd shapes with hard or soft warty shells and are hollow inside.

Cultivars and varieties: Gourds are named for what they look like, such as serpent, spoon, striped pear, caveman's club, dolphin, or nest egg.

Type: Annual

Sun: Full

Soil: Average

Water: Moderate (too much causes gourds to split)

Comments: Choose from several different kinds based on usage.

Harvest: Fall

Uses: Gourds have many craft uses, including birdhouses, dipping utensils, Christmas tree ornaments, and dolls, and can easily be painted for decoration.

ONION (*Allium cepa*)

Description: Onions are either bulbing (large 1–5 inch [3–13 cm] bulb) or bunching (small 1-inch [3 cm] tuber). Bulbs come in green, red, purple, yellow, or white.

ONION *(continued)*

Cultivars: 'Burgundy' has bright red skin and flesh marked with white rings; 'Stockton Red' has thick, dark purple skin.

Type: Annual
Sun: Full
Soil: Light, rich, neutral, well drained (will not grow well in clay soils)
Water: Ample
Harvest: Summer or fall
Uses: Onions are used for many types of cooking; the skins can be used to make dye.

PEPPERS *(Capsicum varieties)*

Description: Peppers show tremendous variety and are available in all shapes, colors, and sizes. The fruit forms from a small white flower that appears on a small, bushy annual plant. Peppers are either sweet or hot. Long, narrow peppers are usually hot, though not always.

Cultivars: 'Bell Boy' is an excellent bell pepper with thick walls and sweet taste. 'Long Red Cayenne' is good for using fresh or dried; it is hot. 'Red Chili' is about 2½ inches (6 cm) long and is very hot.

Type: Annual
Sun: Full
Soil: Rich, moist and well drained, slightly acidic
Water: Low
Harvest: Sweet varieties should be picked before they mature completely, hot varieties after they are fully mature.
Uses: Flavoring, cooking, dried pepper wreaths, vegetable strings

Shrubs and Trees

Apple · Boxwood · Holly · Hydrangea · Juniper · Nandina · Rhododendron

---

APPLE *(Malus sp.)*

Description: Apple trees grow 30–40 feet (9-12 m) tall, with rounded crowns and showy pinkish-white blossoms. Leaves are 2–3 inches (5-8 cm) long.

Cultivars and varieties: There are three main groups—Delicious, Jonathan, and McIntosh. Granny Smith, originally from Australia and New Zealand, is a very hard apple and is good for apple-head dolls, for pies, and for tart eating. Red Delicious is good for eating and cooking.

Type: Perennial
Sun: Full
Soil: Rich in organic matter, well drained
Water: Ample
Comments: Staking and pruning are usually necessary.
Harvest: Gather ripe fruit in fall.
Uses: The fruit can be used for apple-head dolls, apple butter and jelly, pies, cakes, and more.

BOXWOOD *(Buxus sempervirens)*

Description: This evergreen shrub with small, shiny leaves and inconspicuous flowers can grow to 20 feet (6 m) or more.

Cultivars and varieties: *Suffruticosa* is a dwarf form that grows 3 feet (1 m) tall; *arborescens* is a conical form.

Type: Perennial
Sun: Full sun or partial shade
Soil: Rich, moist, well drained
Water: Average
Harvest: Any time during growing season

Uses: Use fresh in topiary, evergreen wreaths, and arrangements.

HOLLY *(Ilex latifolia)*

Description: This evergreen shrub can grow 50 feet (15 m) tall and produces bright berries in late fall. The edges of the leathery leaves are marked by spiny teeth.

Cultivars: 'Nellie Stevens' has dark green leaves and will produce berries without a male plant.

Type: Perennial

Sun: Full

Soil: Rich, moist, well drained

Water: Average

Harvest: Berries in late fall and winter, leaves any time during growing season

Uses: Holly works well in evergreen wreaths, in arrangements, or waxed for decoration.

HYDRANGEA *(Hydrangea macrophylla)*

Description: A rounded, deciduous shrub, hydrangea grows 5–8 feet (1.5–2 m) tall and spreads 6–10 feet (2–3 m). It bears large clusters of blue, pink, or white flowers and oval, bright green leaves.

Cultivars: 'Annabelle' has huge white flower heads; 'Otaksa' is bright blue; 'Forever Pink' is bright pink.

Type: Perennial

Sun: Full or light shade

Soil: Tolerates average soil; pH determines flower color: acidic produces blue, alkaline results in pink.

Water: Moderate

Harvest: Collect blossoms as they begin to dry and turn crisp.

Uses: Fresh flowers in arrangements; dried for wreaths, box gardens, tussie-mussies, potpourri, and Christmas ornaments

---

JUNIPER *(Juniperus communis)*

Description: Juniper comes in a great variety of sizes and shapes and grows from 8 to 75 feet (2–23 m) tall. Foliage is generally evergreen, with needlelike leaves.

Cultivars and species: *J. communis* is 8–12 feet (2–4 m) tall; *J. chinensis* is used as ground cover.

Type: Perennial

Sun: Full

Soil: Acidic or neutral, good drainage

Water: Average

Comments: Prune low branches in spring to stimulate new growth.

Harvest: Any time during growing season

Uses: Fresh juniper is ideal for evergreen wreaths, arrangements, or tied in a bundle for a barbecue wand. Dried works well in hot pads, bath bags, and potpourri.

NANDINA *(Nandina domestica)*

Description: This shrub grows 6–8 feet (2–2.5 m) tall and 2 feet (60 cm) wide, with white flowers in late spring and large clusters of bright red berries in fall and winter. The narrow leaves turn bright red in fall. Dwarf forms are also available.

NANDINA *(continued)*

Type: Perennial
Sun: Full or light shade
Soil: Rich, well drained
Water: Moderate
Harvest: Berries in winter; leaves any time during growing season
Uses: Berries are excellent for holiday decorations.

RHODODENDRON *(Rhododendron sp.)*

Description: Medium to large shrubs, rhododendrons have large cup-shaped flowers borne at the tips of branches. Rhododendron leaves occur in whorls and are long, leathery, and generally much larger than the leaves of azaleas (which are also classified botanically as *Rhododendron.)*

Cultivars and species: *R. angustinii* is native to North America, grows 6 feet (2 m) tall, and has blue or purple blossoms 2–2½ inches (5–6 cm) across. *R. catawbiense* grows 6–8 feet (2–2.5 m) tall with white to pinkish flowers appearing late spring or early summer. *R. chapmanii* grows 6–8 feet (2–2.5 m) tall and has clear pale pink flowers 2–3 inches (5–8 cm) across. *R. carolinianum* and *R. catawbiense* are native shrubs.

Type: Shrub
Sun: Partial or full shade
Water: Moderate; protect from drying winds
Harvest: Blossoms should be picked just before they are fully opened.
Uses: Fresh rhododendron works well in floral arrangements, in May Day baskets, on spring hats, or as pressed blossoms.

Appendixes

Lists of Crafts

&

Special Occasions

BRIDAL SHOWER
Bath Bags
Bath Oils
Bride's Book of Flowers
Dried-Flower Strings
Handmade Paper and Scented Ink
Pressed-Flower Place Cards
Pressed-Flower Picture
Pot of Larkspur
Rosebud Napkin Ring
Rose Perfume
Rose Soap
Sachets
Scented Pot Holders
Tussie-mussies
Wheat and Roses

CHRISTMAS
Apple-Head Dolls (dressed as Santa)
Corn-Shuck Dolls (angel variation)
Cranberry-Basil Jelly
Evergreen Wreath
Gourd Doll
Herb Wreath Bell Pull
Miniature Ornaments
Miniature Terrariums
Moss-Covered Box
Naturally Dyed Cloth
Rose and Boxwood Topiary

Scented Pot Holders (with pine-needle stuffing)
Ten Tiny Trinkets
Whole Wheat Basil Bread

MOTHER'S DAY
Bath Bags or Bath Oils
Flavored Cooking Oils
Floral Hat
Handmade Paper and Scented Ink
Herbal or Lavender Vinegars
Herbal Tea
Garden in a Box
Moss-Covered Box
Pressed-Flower Picture
Rose Perfume or Rose Soap
Sachets
Scented Pot Holders
Violet Jelly
Violet-Jelly Shortbread

FATHER'S DAY
Gourd Birdhouse
Herbal Tea
Miniature Terrariums
Moss-Covered Box
Peach Bread
Peach Jam
Pesto Sauce
Salsa
Seeds from the Garden
Whole Wheat Basil Bread

Housewarming Presents

Bouquet Garni
Cranberry-Basil Jelly
Dried Herbs
Flavored Cooking Oils
Gourd Birdhouse
Herbal and Lavender Vinegars
Herb Wreath Bell Pull
Sachets
Scented Pot Holders
Seeds from the Garden
Vegetable Strings
Violet Jelly
Windowsill Herbs

Types of Crafts

Baskets and Boxes
Baby Basket
Garden in a Box
Herb Box
May Day Basket
Moss-Covered Box
Wheelbarrow Baskets of Herbs
Woven Herb Basket

Dolls and Dollhouse Accessories
Apple-Head Dolls
Corn-Shuck Dolls
Dollhouse Garden
Flower Basket Ornament
Gourd Doll
Straw-Hat Ornament
Tussie-mussie Ornament

Food

Bouquet Garni
Cranberry-Basil Jelly
Deep-Dish Apple Pie
Flavored Cooking Oils
Herbal Tea
Herbal Vinegars
Peach Bread
Peach Jam
Pesto Sauce
Pickled Peaches
Salsa
Violet Jelly
Violet-Jelly Shortbread
Whole Wheat Basil Bread

Herbal Products

Bath Bags
Bouquet Garni
Dried Herbs
Herbal Tea
Herbal Vinegar
Herb Box
Herb Wreath Bell Pull
Potpourri
Sachets
Scented Pot Holders
Wheelbarrow Baskets of Herbs
Windowsill Herbs
Woven Herb Basket

TABLE DECOR

Daisy Topiary Bear
Easter Egg Hunt Centerpiece
May Day Basket
Pot of Larkspur
Pressed-Flower Place Cards
Rose and Boxwood Topiary
Rosebud Napkin Ring
Scented Pot Holders
Wheat and Roses
Wheelbarrow Baskets of Herbs
Woven Herb Basket

VICTORIANA

Dried-Flower Strings
Floral Hat
Handmade Paper and Scented Ink
Moss-Covered Box
Potpourri
Pressed-Flower Place Cards
Pressed-Flower Picture
Rose and Boxwood Topiary
Rosebud Napkin Ring
Rose Perfume
Rose Soap
Sachets
Straw-Hat, Tussie-mussie,
and Flower Basket Ornaments
Tussie-mussies
Violet Jelly

LEAST EXPENSIVE

Apple-Head Dolls
Bath Bags
Bouquet Garni
Cranberry-Basil Jelly
Dried-Flower Strings
Gourd Projects
Herb Wreath Bell Pull
Miniature Ornaments
Miniature Terrariums
Moss-Covered Box
Peach Bread
Pesto Sauce
Potpourri
Rose Soap
Sachets
Salsa
Scented Pot Holders
Seeds from the Garden
Ten Tiny Trinkets
Tussie-mussies
Vegetable Strings
Violet Jelly
Whole Wheat Basil Bread

QUICKEST TO MAKE

Bath Bags
Bath Oil
Bouquet Garni
Flavored Cooking Oils
Gourd Spoons
Miniature Ornaments
Sachets
Ten Tiny Trinkets
Tussie-mussies

Sources of Supplies

&

Dorothy Biddle Service
U.S. Route 6
Greeley, PA 18425-9799
(717) 226-3239
Flower-arranging supplies

Caprilands Herb Farm
Silver Street
Coventry, CT 06238
(203) 742-7244
Topiary, wreaths, potpourri, dried herbs and flowers

The Corn Crib
R.R. 2, Box 109
Madison, MI 65263
(314) 682-2002
Corn shucks, corn silk, and other shuck-craft supplies

Country House Floral Supply
P.O. Box 4086 BVL Station
Andover, MA 01810
(508) 475-8463
Flower-arranging supplies

Iden Croft Herbs
Frittenden Road
Staplehurst, Kent
England TN12 ODH
(44 580) 891432
Potted herbs, potpourri, dried flowers

Irene's Topiary
3045 North Academy
Sanger, CA 93657
(209) 875-8447
Topiary frames, planted and stuffed topiary

Lindemann AG Co.
2817 West Locust Avenue
Fresno, CA 93711
(209) 449-1230
Freeze-dried flowers

Meadowbrook Farm
1633 Washington Lane
Meadowbrook, PA 19046
(215) 887-5900
Frames and moss-filled forms

Naomi's Herbs
11 Housatonic Street
Lenox, MA 01240
(413) 637-0616
Dried herbs, spices, and flowers

Topiary, Inc.
41 Bering Road
Tampa, FL 33606
(813) 254-3229
Wire topiary frames

Selected Bibliography

Brooklyn Botanic Garden. *Handbook on Dye Plants and Dyeing.* New York, 1986. A small but useful publication on various dye plants and how to grow and use them.

Buchanan, Rita. *A Weaver's Garden.* Loveland, Col.: Interweave Press, 1987. An excellent guide to growing various plants for natural dyes.

Cameron, Julia. *The Artist's Way.* New York: Perigee, Putnam Publishing Group, 1992. An invaluable workbook for learning to believe in your art and your creativity.

Foster, Maureen. *The Flower Arranger's Encyclopedia of Preserving and Drying.* London: Blandford, 1988. A guide to drying fruits, flowers, and foliage plants.

Gallup, Barbara, and Deborah Reich. *The Complete Book of Topiary.* New York: Workman Publishing, 1987. A good basic guide to topiary; coverage includes stuffed and planted topiaries, mock topiary, and instructions for making your own frames.

Hill, Madalene, and Gwen Barclay. *Southern Herb Growing.* Fredericksburg, Tex.: Shearer Publishing, 1987. A must for growing herbs in the South. Includes growing information as well as many recipes.

Hillier, Malcolm. *Decorating with Dried Flowers.* New York: Crown Publishers, 1987. A step-by-step guide to growing, drying, and using various dried flowers.

Kollath, Richard. *Wreaths.* Boston: Houghton Mifflin Co., 1988. Clear directions for making some creative and interesting wreaths.

Kowalchik, Claire, and William H. Hylton, eds. *Rodale's Illustrated Encyclopedia of Herbs.* Emmaus, Penn.: Rodale Press, 1987. An excellent sourcebook for growing and using all the common herbs.

Macqueen, Sheila. *Flower Arranging from Your Garden.* Radnor, Penn.: Chilton Book Company, 1977. A guide to growing plants useful in floral arrangements.

Martin, Laura C. *Garden Flower Folklore.* Chester, Conn.: Globe Pequot Press, 1987. A guide to legends and symbols of one hundred garden flowers.

——. *Wildflower Folklore.* Chester, Conn.: Globe Pequot Press, 1983. A guide to legends and symbols of one hundred wildflowers.

Newdick, Jane. *Betty Crocker's Book of Flowers.* New York: Prentice Hall, 1989. A lovely book giving suggestions for using flowers in cooking and decorating.

Oster, Maggie. *Gifts and Crafts from the Garden.* Emmaus, Penn.: Rodale Press, 1988. A very good book on basic garden crafts. Clear instructions and attractive black-and-white drawings.

Pulleyn, Rob. *The Wreath Book.* New York: Sterling Publishing Co., 1988. Directions for making over one hundred kinds of wreaths. Good, easy-to-use book that includes many wreaths made of flowers and other natural materials.

Sanders, Jewel. *Keep on Shuckin'.* Moberly, Mich.: Crown Press, 1981. A guide to various corn-shuck crafts.

Shaudys, Phyllis V. *The Pleasures of Herbs.* Pownal, Vt.: Garden Way Publishing, 1986. A month-by-month listing of herbal gifts, including many recipes and some unusual and fun crafts.

Tolley, Emelie, and Chris Mead. *Gifts from the Herb Garden.* New York: Clarkson Potter, 1991. Instructions for many herbal crafts including beauty products, wreaths, and topiaries.

——. *The Herbal Pantry.* New York: Clarkson Potter, 1992. A beautiful book that includes many culinary herbal recipes.

Index

❧